Autism spectrum condition and Asperger syndrome

What to do when you don't know what to do!

A practical early intervention toolkit for families

Written by Josie Edwards

Illustrated by Jerry Carter

Dedicated to all the families quietly getting on with supporting loved ones every day.

Also a special thank you to Anna for holding our hands throughout the writing of this book.

Editor: Anna Davidson

First published 2017 by MadeByEducators Ltd, London

Every effort has been made to ensure that the information in this book is complete and accurate. However, neither the publisher nor the author is engaged in rendering professional advice or services to the individual reader. The ideas, procedures and suggestions contained in this book are not intended as a substitute for consulting with your healthcare provider. Neither the publishers nor the author shall be liable or responsible for any loss or damage allegedly arising from any information or suggestion in this book.

Text copyright © 2017 Josie Edwards
Illustrations copyright © 2017 Jerry Carter

All Rights Reserved. The moral rights of the author have been asserted.
Resources in this book may be photocopied for personal use by parents or teachers.

ISBN-13: 978-0-9956748-0-6
ISBN-10: 0995674809

A CIP catalogue record for this book is available from the British Library.

Extracts from 'The Reason I Jump: one boy's voice from the silence of autism' by Naoki Higashida reproduced by permission of Hodder and Stoughton Limited.

www.madebyeducators.com

Contents

Introduction   7
    Why we wrote this book
    A research-based approach
    Developing a team approach
    Professional input is essential
    A 'building block' approach to interventions

Chapter 1. What is autism?   15
    Developmental delay and Asperger syndrome
    Sensory issues
    Anxiety

Chapter 2. Join me in my world   23
    Be the most interesting thing in the room
    You are an important person in my world
    Echolalia
    Repetition
    Extend my interactions with you
    Encouraging interaction (verbal and non-verbal)
    Want to learn more?

Chapter 3. Understand my sensory profile   35
    Filtering sensory information
    Sensory issues: impact on anxiety and behaviour
    Stimming
    To stim or not to stim?
    Stimming and the senses
    Understand your child's sensory needs using a sensory checklist
    My sensory profile
    Sensory DIet
    Building a 'day-to-day', a sensory toolkit
    Example sensory diet
    A wider world of senses
    Experiencing the world very differently
    Want to learn more?

Chapter 4. Support my brain development through movement   59
    'Crossing the midline'
    Hypermobility
    Building functional motor skills
    Want to learn more?

Chapter 5. Motivate me   67
    Special interests as motivators
    Reward charts
    Beyond the Star Chart
    Want to learn more?

Chapter 6. Motivation and technology   85
    Why technology?
    Screen time and overstimulation
    Technology time as a social time
    Want to learn more?

Chapter 7. My visual world   95
    Now and Next Boards
    Visual timetables
    Visual sequencing
    Want to learn more?

Chapter 8. Help me learn to manage my emotions   113
    Teach emotional self-regulation
    Step 1. Identifying feelings
    Move on to introduce a wide range of emotions
    Step 2. Where in your body are you feeling that emotion?
    Step 3. Identify the strength of feelings
    Step 4. Develop strategies to manage the emotion in the body
    Don't forget to breathe
    Eventually you will be able to use these skills together
    Mindfulness
    Want to learn more?

Chapter 9. Help me to develop social skills   **143**
    Help me learn through playdates
    Playdate planner
    Friendship skills
    Be a good friend
    Playdates and technology
    Want to learn more?

Chapter 10. Encouraging self-knowledge   **163**
    Developing a positive sense of self
    Examples of normalizing differences and encouraging self-knowledge
    Building on strengths
    Introducing your child to their diagnosis
    Developing an 'Aspie' identity
    Want to learn more?

Chapter 11. Teach me theory of mind   **169**
    The false belief test
    Supporting development of theory of mind
    Activities to raise awareness of theory of mind issues
    Cartoon communication
    Expected and unexpected behaviour
    Films to support understanding of theory of mind
    Want to learn more?

Chapter 12. Care for the carers   **193**
    The process of adapting to the ASC diagnosis
    Take one day at a time
    Build a support network
    Want to learn more?

References   **201**

About the author and illustrator   **203**

Introduction

If there were one 'right' approach to supporting children with developmental delays and autism spectrum condition (ASC) we would all be using it!

The reality is that there are many approaches, some of them making grand claims and requiring specialist support as well as a great deal of parents' time and money. It takes time to research and understand what your child needs and how to access that support, but please don't delay – your child needs early intervention now.

We have written a practical guide to a range of family-friendly, free strategies designed to help you support your child today. We have taken a highly visual approach to information in this book as it models the strategies widely recommended for kids on the spectrum.

This book has been written as a sequence of overlapping early interventions. The first few interventions are crucial for children at the earlier developmental stages; later strategies are more suitable for children further along the developmental timeline.

Here is a toolkit of strategies that can be implemented straight away. These strategies do not require training and, importantly, can be a fun part of everyday family life.

Why we wrote this book

When families suspect that their child needs additional support, the term 'early intervention' is often used, but not always well understood. Families can spend years working their way through the maze of research and interventions and no one should have to feel as lost and helpless as we did during such a critical time.

Having spent the last six years researching and living early intervention strategies we have written the book that we would have liked to have received back when we started. With the help of educators, parents and children, we have written a guide that should be easy to access for people with very little time. We have sifted through the research and picked out the most family-friendly, evidence-based strategies. We have also avoided expensive therapy routes and focused on what the family can do at home, for free, straight away. It's a steep learning curve, but so rewarding when things work. Good luck on your journey.

A research-based approach

Research into autism interventions is difficult as children with autism are all so very different. They will often have several interventions at once and denying a child an intervention in order to create a control group could be quite unethical. It can be very hard for researchers to single out which strategy was responsible for any improvement. The British National Autistic Society in the UK and the Autism Society of America both have excellent websites offering research-based wider information, resources and numerous conferences for parents.

The UK charity Research Autism[1] is also an excellent resource for giving guidance and ruling out the potentially harmful strategies (unfortunately there are some!). As with most of the resources we came to rely upon, it took us some time to stumble across this particular one, and I recommend that every parent have a look early on. We summarise their verdict on each strategy at the end of each chapter.

Developing a team approach

You may have heard the proverb,

> 'It takes a village to raise a child.'

Since becoming the parent of a child with special needs I now think of it more as,

> 'It takes an informed village to raise an autistic child.'

Your child needs your support, and as they grow their team (village) will grow too, to include their teachers, their classmates and their school community. Closer to home, their team is likely to include parents or legal guardians, grandparents, aunts and uncles, and even family friends.

Intervention strategies can be agreed, shared and applied by anyone in your child's team.

Professional input is essential

Occupational and speech therapy are the cornerstones of interventions. If you suspect developmental delay, make an appointment with your doctor today and take all the help you can get. Although based on research the information in this toolkit has been written by teachers and parents who do not have medical training. Professional therapy can be difficult to access, so this book provides harmless, research-based strategies to be used by untrained parents at home.

The strategies in this book are designed to support, not replace, the relationship that exists between you and your healthcare providers as professional input is essential.

Most families' experience of diagnosis includes shock at how little support there is out there. Do fight for and accept all the professional advice and support that you can get, but don't delay intervention.
Don't just wait for the professionals to turn up with therapy; you might be waiting a very long time, and your child needs support now.

A 'building block' approach to interventions

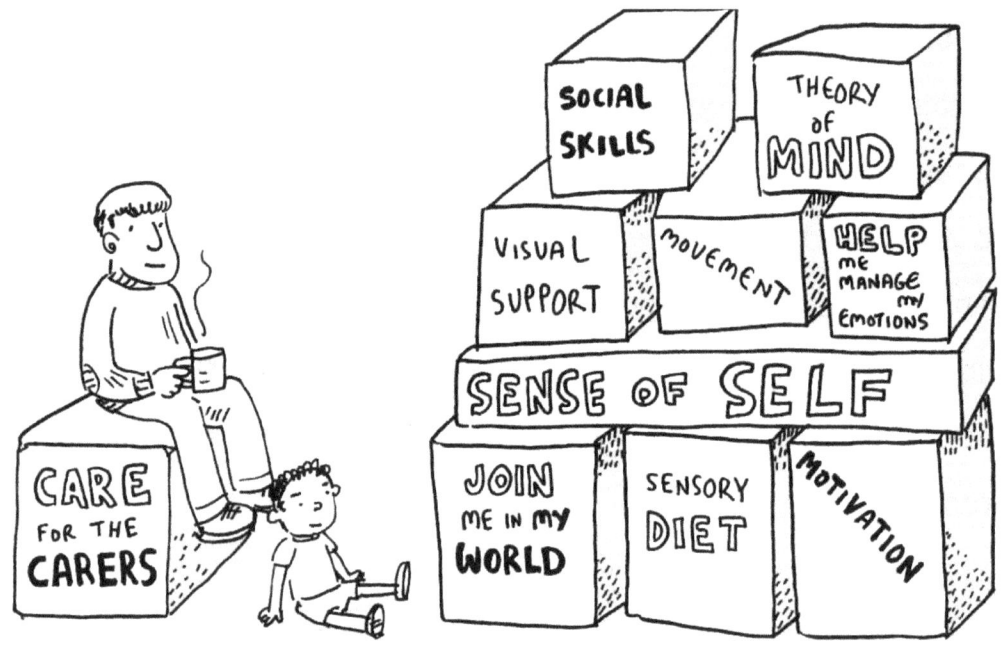

All children grow and change, and an intervention can be grown into or out of, so we have structured this book with a bit of a timeline in mind. Children need to have developed some engagement and motivation before things like managing emotions and developing social skills can be supported effectively.

As engagement is a basic foundation for other interventions, *Join me in my world* is an obvious early chapter. Understanding your child's *sensory profile* allows you to consider the world from their perspective and to develop strategies to reduce their stress. *Visual support*, *motivation* and *managing emotions,* covered in Chapters 5-8, will be important at all stages of their development.

Activities like 'Now and Next Boards' (see p96), timelines and reward systems are useful as soon as possible as they help make day-to-day life work. It's hard to have energy for games if your child won't even put their socks on! The reward systems may fade away as your child gets older but the visual strategies may well be with your child into adulthood. Remember: we all have systems, such as diaries, apps, calendars and so on, that we use to help us organize our lives. Our children will grow into using these same tools too.

We move on to *social skills* and *theory of mind,* which both build upon the earlier chapters. *Encouraging self-knowledge* has children aged 7 and above in mind. Having insight into and acceptance of differences links into protecting mental health, which is something to consider at this early age so that you can put strategies in place to help kids before they encounter the many challenges that adolescence brings.

Chapter 1
What is autism?

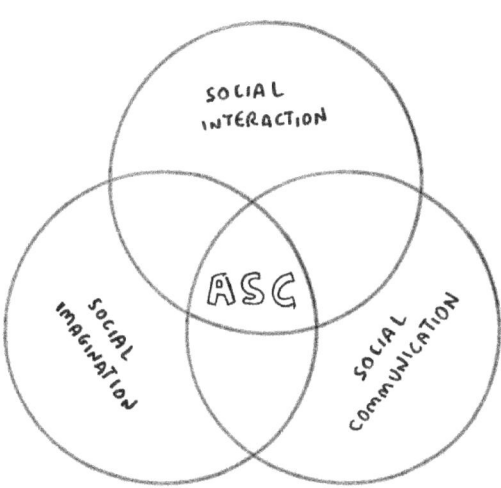

More than 1 in 100 people are on the autistic spectrum. Autism is a lifelong developmental condition that affects the way in which people experience the world around them. Whilst every person experiences autism in a unique way there are many shared difficulties.

Social interaction and communication can be particularly difficult for people on the autistic spectrum due to difficulties with processing language and difficulties in imagining what others are thinking or feeling. An autism diagnosis also indicates obsessions and repetitive behaviours and interests.

In a child with classic autism the presence of a delay in language during early development is typical, whereas this is not the case for a child who has high-functioning autism or Asperger syndrome. Both high-functioning autism and Asperger syndrome can be understood and supported in a similar way.

Autism is a spectrum condition and every child is unique so a diagnosis can feel frustrating as it might not clearly fit your particular child.

There is an abundance of information explaining what autism is according to the diagnostic criteria, but we wrote this book because there is much less information about how to thrive with autism. We hope that this book will help ASC families to adapt, to accept, and to grow.

Developmental delay and Asperger syndrome

Developmental delays are not necessarily caused by lifelong physical and mental conditions. They may be signs of hearing, learning or attention issues and early intervention can often help kids catch up.

Developmental delays can be the first sign to a family that their child is struggling. Delays in speech in a child around the age of 2 are often a trigger for families to raise concerns with their doctor, but families may have other concerns well before then.

As this is an EARLY intervention toolkit it is something that can be used by parents who suspect that their child needs help and want to start intervention as soon as possible. A diagnosis of any developmental condition can take years, and it is so important to start intervention, even if you are only slightly concerned.

The term Asperger syndrome has now been replaced diagnostically with high-functioning autism (HFA), however we have used it in this book as it is a term that is still widely used today, and is fairly well understood by the general population. The key message here is that both Asperger syndrome and high-functioning autism present themselves in largely the same way, and can be treated with identical strategies.

Classic autism can be thought of as an array of co-existing developmental delays. Classic autism needs a much stronger emphasis on language development than Asperger syndrome, but that language work can only be effective when the same core building blocks are in place.

For all these conditions, the key challenges are engagement, motivation, sensory issues, movement and managing the frustrations that being different brings.

If you are worried about your child's development there is so much that you can do. A developmental delay may well be just that and your child may catch up without additional support. However, I have yet to meet a family of a special needs child who does not have some regrets about not having started to help them sooner.

Strategies are play-based, so at worst interventions are fun games for your family, and at best they are immediate therapy for your struggling child.

Sensory issues

We have dedicated the whole of Chapter 3, *Understand my sensory profile* to exploring your child's possible sensory issues. Sensory issues impact so significantly on some children's lives that we are highlighting them here as well.

As non-spectrum, 'neurotypical', kids grow they become increasingly able to focus their attention on a particular sense while reducing attention paid to others.

ASC kids often have less control over their sensory input and may get too much or too little 'feedback' from certain senses, which can be enormously distracting.

We have included a sensory checklist in this book to enable you to get an overview of your child's sensory profile and gain a deeper insight into their world.

Anxiety

Our kids are working twice as hard as everyone else every day. When you consider what they have to deal with – the sensory distractions, the effort needed to focus attention, the constant puzzle of what it is that they are supposed to be doing – our kids start to look like heroes. The anxiety that this uncertainty can bring, particularly the social anxiety, can be a debilitating consequence of autism and it is something that we can reduce.

Once the sensory and anxiety issues are understood the more challenging behaviour, such as the meltdowns, avoidance or repetitive behaviour and the need for routine, all begin to make sense and we can develop real understanding and compassion for their situation.

All the strategies in this pack involve helping a child with anxiety, as follows:

- Building a sensory profile helps a family to reduce stressful experiences.
- Creating a sensory diet helps children to self-regulate their sensory world.
- Timetables help kids know and prepare for what is coming next.

- Star Charts let kids know which behaviours are helpful and which should be reduced.
- Tuning into emotions will eventually lead to better self-management of difficult emotions.

And remember:

if you've met one child with autism, you've met ONE child with autism.

All our children are unique human beings who will vary in such enormous ways. This book lays out an array of strategies, some of which will work wonderfully with your child, and others of which might not be the right approach at this developmental stage.

Make the most of any support you are offered by your healthcare providers. **The strategies in this toolkit are only to be used in conjunction with, not as a replacement for, professional advice.**

All these strategies and resources are considered 'best practice' in the ASC teaching world and we have only included strategies that have worked well for us. The resources in this pack are designed to be family-friendly, for instant use, and do not require costly therapies or training, so it's worth a go!

Chapter 2
Join me in my world

Many children on the autistic spectrum have difficulty filtering out distractions in their environment (more on this in Chapter 3). Parents can struggle to get the attention of their child. Copying their behaviour can gain attention, build bonds and be a crucial start to understanding your child's world. A 'low sensory' (simple and uncluttered) environment will reduce distractions, helping your child to focus on you.

Be the most interesting thing in the room

A very talented speech and language therapist gave me a gem of advice in the early days: 'You need to be the most interesting thing in the room!'. Visually entertaining, unexpected or novel experiences are more likely to gain your child's attention.

Follow my interests

Take advantage of your child's interests in the world around them (their 'milieu'). Use their interests to gain attention and expand their communication through the things that interest them (see more on this in Chapters 5 and 6 on motivation).

You are an important person in my world

Trying to engage a child who does not respond can be a frustrating activity. Autism can get in the way of so many developmental experiences, including bonding. Love and engagement are essential to the developmental process. It will take time and perseverance but every breakthrough is so very rewarding. You get to strengthen your bond with your child, your child gets a really responsive playmate (you), and once your connection strengthens, which it will, it can be so much fun.

Engaging activities

- Blowing bubbles
- Peek-a-boo
- Looking at books
- Jigsaws
- Petting animals
- Swimming pool games involving looking at each other
- Playing with balloons
- Hiding a biscuit and asking, 'Where has the biscuit gone?'
- Using an iPad together e.g. two-player games.

Echolalia

It's very easy to miss an autistic child's early attempts to communicate with you. Echolalia is a good example. Echolalia is the repetition of speech by a child learning to talk. Here is an example of one form of echolalia.

Dad discussing his concerns for his child with a friend.

Dad: He doesn't answer questions – there is something not right about his development.

Friend: He looks fine to me.

Dad: No, let me show you. Johnnie, would you like an apple or an orange?

Johnnie: Orange.

Friend: See, he's fine.

Dad: No, I'll show you. Johnnie, would you like an orange or an apple?

Johnnie: Apple.

Friend: Oh!

Although it can initially be worrying, echolalia is a good sign that a child is attempting to communicate. They are struggling with communicating effectively, but they are trying. Repeating back the last word spoken to them or using phrases from television programmes are all attempts to engage.

Repetition

A child may repeat the same question or phrase over and over again. This is in order both to reduce anxiety by getting the same answer repeatedly and to try to maintain some form of dialogue.

Repetition of a question could also be a way of processing the question.

This is well expressed by Naoki, a 13-year-old boy with autism:

Firing the question back is a way of sifting through our memories to pick up clues about what the question was asking. We understand the question okay but can't answer it until we fish the right memory pictures in our heads.

Naoki Higashida, *The Reason I Jump*[9]

Echolalia and repetition are both positive signs as they are attempts by the child to communicate. The family can use and work with these to develop, extend and motivate further communication.

Extend my interactions with you

Every time your child engages with you, no matter how simply, they are developing their social communication. Every time you respond positively you have had a cycle of interaction which you can build upon. Cycles of interaction can be verbal or non-verbal.

Many families get too caught up in thinking that autism is mostly about language. Protecting your relationship with your child and building cycles of non-verbal interactions are important in their own right.

What to do when you don't know what to do!

Encouraging interaction (verbal and non-verbal)

How many 'cycles of interaction' can your child sustain?

One cycle of interaction:
1. – Would you like a drink?
   - Yes.

Two cycles of interaction:
1. – Would you like a drink?
   - Yes.
2. – Apple juice or orange?
   - Orange, please.

Three cycles of interaction:
1. – Would you like a drink?
   - Yes.
2. – Apple juice or orange?
   - Orange, please.
3. – Could you get me the cup?
   - Here you are.

These cycles of interactions are signs that your child is engaging and developing more and more all the time. You are likely to be starting with getting needs met; try to stretch these interactions to encourage your child to extend their communication to wider topics.

Want to learn more?

All these activities come under the umbrella of 'developmental interventions' and the National Institute for Health and Care Excellence (NICE) guidelines note that there are likely to be some benefits and there are definitely no risks associated with developmental interventions.

Floortime

Also known as the DIR method: involves the adult as a fun, spontaneous playmate who is happy to follow the child's lead and interests.

Research Autism view:

There is limited research evidence on the use of the DIR method (floortime) as a treatment for autistic children. Because of this we cannot recommend its use, although further large scale, high-quality research into this intervention might be warranted.

Research Autism[2]

Our experience:

We didn't faithfully follow a floortime programme, but did learn a lot from joining our child's world/taking his lead in activities even if it was just lying on the floor! It improved connectedness and could be fun!

Milieu training

Milieu training involves using your child's interests in the world around them as fun learning opportunities (see also p74).

Research Autism view:

There is some limited research evidence to suggest that milieu training has positive effects – usually on children's communication abilities but also in reducing aberrant behaviour.

Research Autism[3]

Our experience:

This was one of the biggest breakthroughs. We were able to join our child's world through his love of windmills, Minecraft, and more recently, computer programming.

Intensive interaction

Intensive interaction involves gaining the attention of your child and developing and expanding natural conversations.

Research Autism view:

One of the most important things an individual learns through the process is that other people are good to be with and that other people enjoy being with them.

Research Autism[4]

Our experience:

Every now and again I count the rounds of communication my son is having. I remember clearly when it was a breakthrough to have two or three. Now (if it's a topic he likes) I can lose count. How can talking to your child ever be a bad thing!

PACT (Super parenting)

Many interventions can sound very much like 'just good parenting' and it can be hard to accept ideas you may have already tried again and again.

But a parenting course can give you the 'super parent' powers that you really need. Research from Professor Green from the University of Manchester[5] into the effectiveness of a preschool autism communication trial (PACT)[5], found that giving parents the skills to become 'super parents' can dramatically improve their child's autism.

We're taking the parent's interaction with the child and taking it to a 'super' level, these children need more than 'good enough', they need something exceptional.

Dr Catherine Aldred[6]

Parents taking part in the study said:

I realise the importance of understanding what he understands and making my communication directly relevant to the context of the interaction. It's a real partnership where we discuss the meaning of his communication and I always go away understanding him so much better with insight.

Parent[7]

You're being really skilled-up by these people who trust your judgement about what makes your child tick.

Louisa Harrison[6]

Our experience:

We were worried that the parenting sessions would be patronising. Our neurotypical child thrived with our far from perfect parenting and it felt at times as if we were being blamed for our autistic child's behaviour as we were not 'good enough' parents. However, the Early Bird[8] sessions by the National Autistic Society (NAS) made a massive positive difference. Our autistic child does need a level of professional parenting that we were not providing, and having clear, structured systems allows our lives to work and allows us to all 'tune into' and enjoy each other as a family.

We also met a lot of other local parents going through the same things and those parents are part of our autism community today!

Sensitive parenting is core to effective intervention and there are unique challenges when trying to 'tune into' an autistic child. This very recent research into 'super parenting' makes total sense to us.

Recommended reading

Greenspan, S. I., *Engaging Autism: Using the Floortime Approach to Help Children Relate, Communicate, and Think* (Merloyd Lawrence, 2009)

Sher, B, *Early Intervention Games: Fun, Joyful Ways to Develop Social and Motor Skills in Children with Autism Spectrum or Sensory Processing Disorders* (Jossey-Bass, 2009)

Pickles, A., Le Couteur, A., Leadbitter, K., et al, 'Parent-mediated social communication therapy for young children with autism (PACT): long-term follow-up of a randomised controlled trial'. *The Lancet* 388 No. 10059 (2016): 2501-2509.

Chapter 3
Understand my sensory profile

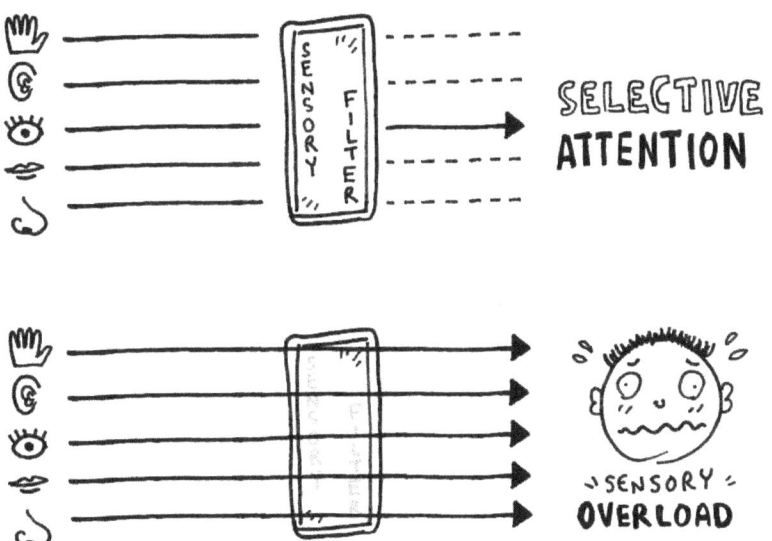

It is common for those with autism to have difficulty regulating their sensory experiences and directing their attention. Completing a sensory checklist will give you a good insight into the difficulties your child may be having in coping with their many senses. Often your child may appear inconsistent, sometimes appearing to need stimulus and sometimes being overloaded.

Sensory issues can involve **dysregulation**. It's not that your child will always be over responsive or under responsive, it's more that they may have difficulty regulating their sensory input. This dysregulation is likely to be more difficult to deal with when your child is tired, unwell or stressed.

Sensory dysregulation can involve:

Difficulty filtering sensory input,

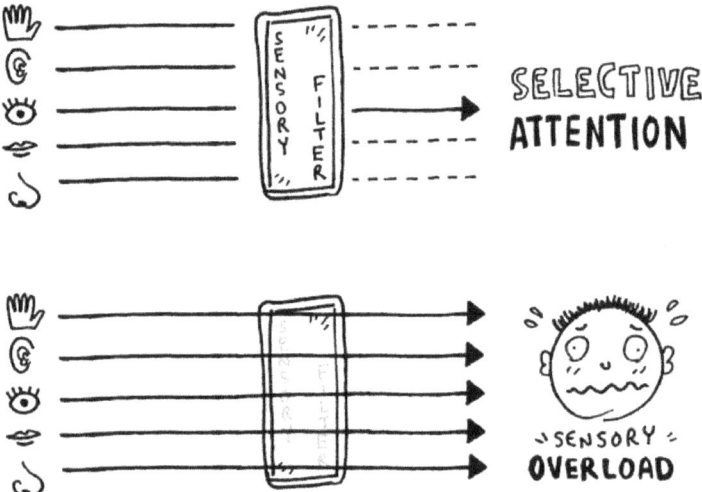

sensory input being blocked,

or sensory input being amplified.

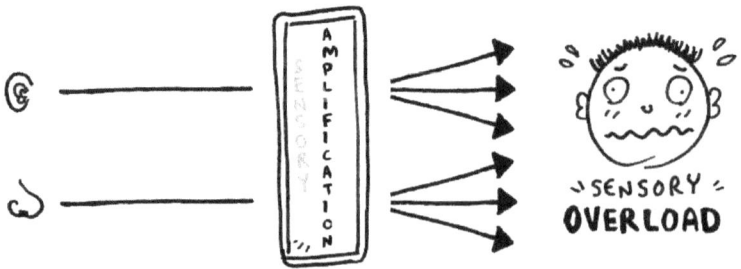

Sensory input diagram concepts courtesy of Dr Prithvi Perepa, University of Northampton.

What to do when you don't know what to do!

Sensory issues: impact on anxiety and behaviour

Sensory input can be distracting...   ...or calming.

Sensory issues can cause overload...   ...or can be managed!

Our children are working harder than their peers just to do day-to-day activities. This will be tiring and brings increased stress to their world. Sensory differences combined with the effort needed to work out what they are supposed to be doing in social situations often create anxiety. Our children can be helped to manage their anxiety. Many of the behaviours associated with autism, such as stimming, are actually examples of self-management of anxiety and sensory issues.

Stimming

'Stimming', or self-stimulatory behaviour, is common in people with autism spectrum condition. Common 'stims' include hand flapping, jumping, eye rolling or staring at lights or shadow patterns.

Some theories suggest that stimming behaviour helps people to regulate their sensory input when being either under or over stimulated.

Other theories suggest that stimming exists to reduce anxiety and sensory overload as it can help to block out over-stimulating environments.

Some suggest that stimming is just very enjoyable:

> *Just watching spinning things fills me with everlasting bliss.*
>
> Naoki Higashida, *The Reason I Jump*[9]

To stim or not to stim?

Stimming behaviour can give us clues to our children's needs and also show us that our children are actively trying to manage their sensory differences in their own way. Some stimming behaviour may place our children in danger. Head banging or behaviour which makes it very difficult to be with other people might need adapting to a safer stim.

An understanding of your child's sensory needs will really help you to support them with their stimming behaviour. Similarly, your child's stims are clues to their sensory needs.

Stimming and the senses

- **Tactile** (touch) – stroking fabric, scratching
- **Smell and taste** – sniffing and mouthing objects
- **Vision** – moving fingers in front of eyes, fascination with lights and shadows, blinking
- **Vestibular/balance** – rocking, swaying
- **Auditory** – repetition of songs, words or sounds, tapping, drumming
- **Proprioception** (body sense in muscles and joints) – jumping, bouncing, squeezing into tight spaces

This is not a fully comprehensive list of senses. To get a fuller picture of your child's sensory profile a sensory checklist is a quick and easy way to gain enormous insight into your child's world.

Understand your child's sensory needs using a sensory checklist

Once you have completed the checklists below enter the totals into 'My Sensory Profile' on p47.

Tactile (touch)	Tick
Avoids light touch.	
Enjoys wrestling games.	
Disturbed by vibration e.g. motorized toys, hand dryers, etc.	
Very fussy about shoes or clothing. May complain that material 'hurts'.	
Does not notice being touched or bumped.	
Finds messy hands or face upsetting.	
Chews or sucks on toys, hands, pencils, clothing, etc.	
Craves or avoids water play.	
Likes a repetitive behaviour e.g. hand flapping, tapping, banging, etc.	
Dislikes or craves particular materials, e.g. silk or paper.	
Total	

What to do when you don't know what to do!

Smell and Taste	Tick
Complains about, or is overexcited by smells.	
Doesn't seem to notice strong odours e.g. paint, markers or strong cheese.	
Mouths or licks objects and people.	
Smells objects and people.	
Picky eating/fussy.	
Shows challenging behaviour around meal times.	
Complains about or is overexcited by tastes.	
Total	

Vision	Tick
Makes poor eye contact.	
Easily overloaded by places with a lot of visual information e.g. a classroom.	
Poor ball skills – catching and/or throwing.	
Struggles to follow moving objects or people.	
Stares at lights or is distracted by different types of lighting.	
Gets distressed or extremely excited when lights are dimmed or it is dark.	
Has difficulty copying, e.g. from pictures or a board.	
Has difficulty with eye-hand coordination, e.g. writing, drawing, threading beads.	
Struggles with reading.	
Squints, blinks, or rubs eyes frequently.	
Displays visual stims, e.g. spinning objects, flapping hands, waving fingers in front of eyes.	
Total	

What to do when you don't know what to do!

Vestibular/Balance	Tick
Seems clumsy and awkward.	
Fidgets constantly.	
Stumbles often, slouches in chair.	
Is excessively cautious on climbing frames or stairs.	
Displays movement stims e.g. likes to run in circles, spin, jump.	
May suddenly fall out of a chair or onto another person.	
Likes to rock, on floor or in a chair.	
Touches everything, e.g. furniture or walls, when walking.	
Avoids changing head position.	
Avoids or craves riding on cars, trains, buses.	
Gets dizzy very easily.	
Total	

Auditory	Tick
Displays auditory stims, e.g. humming, repetitive noises.	
Doesn't seem to hear you.	
Is more relaxed in one-to-one situations than in group settings.	
Prone to tantrums in spaces with unusual acoustics, e.g. halls.	
Has difficulty filtering out noise and focusing on one voice.	
Is distressed by loud noises e.g. sirens, bells, etc.	
Speaks with a voice that does not fit the setting e.g. too loud in a library.	
Complains that things are too loud, or insists on turning things up too loud!	
Disturbed or extremely excited by singing and musical instruments.	
Total	

What to do when you don't know what to do!

Proprioception	Tick
Seems unsure how to move their body in space, almost as if they don't know where body parts are.	
Crashes and falls on purpose.	
Can be very lethargic, seems weak, slumps when sitting/standing.	
Likes deep massage or being 'squished'.	
Bumps into walls, objects, people.	
Tires very easily.	
Has difficulty assessing force needed e.g. slams doors by accident, breaks crayons and pencil points.	
Total	

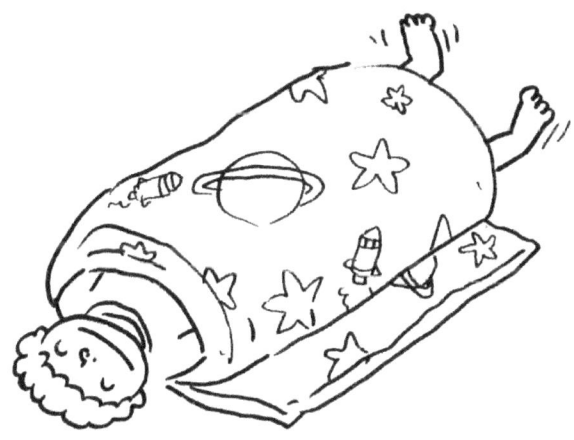

Play involving gentle pressure/squishing.

Behaviour, Learning and Social Issues	Tick
Has difficulty with transitions between activities.	
Likes repetitive play.	
Finds putting things into sequences very difficult.	
Can be demanding or hard to calm down.	
Doesn't understand personal space.	
Craves predictability and is resistant to change in routines.	
Has difficulty joining in with group activities.	
Is easily overwhelmed or frustrated.	
Frequently 'zones out', or withdraws.	
Shows a lack of organization, loses things frequently.	
Can be overly aggressive or passive/withdrawn.	
Has difficulty making friends.	
Total	

My sensory profile

	Typical sensory response	Some sensory issues	Strong sensory issues	Your child's profile
Tactile (touch)	1-2	3-6	7-10	
Smell and Taste	1-2	3-4	5-7	
Vision	1-2	3-6	7-11	
Vestibular/Balance	1-2	3-6	7-11	
Auditory	1-2	3-5	6-9	
Proprioception	1-2	3-4	5-7	
Behaviour, Learning & Social Issues	1-3	4-6	7-12	

If your child scores 'strong sensory issues' in any of the categories there is a lot that you can do to accommodate their sensory sensitivities and help them to self-manage these differences. You will be able to develop a sensory toolkit to help them cope in difficult environments and eventually a sensory diet can become a fun part of everyday family time.

Sensory diet

A sensory diet includes a range of activities built into a child's daily routine to help them to self-regulate, reduce overload, and allow them to pay more attention to the world around them.

A sensory diet would be prescribed by an occupational therapist and if you can access that kind of support then do. The strategies in this book are not designed to replace professional advice and we recommend getting as much professional support as possible.

The following is an outline of what a sensory diet might look like and gives you some idea of what you, and your family, can do at home, today, to support your child's sensory needs.

Tactile (touch)

Deep pressure (bear hugs), back rubs, brushing, soft fabrics for clothing, removing tags from clothing, water play, finger painting, weighted blankets, encouraging working with mud pies/play putty/dough, climbing under sofa cushions, gentle wrestling.

Smell, taste and oral

Adding or removing scented candles, blindfolded smelling games, activities exploring tastes or textures, sucking through straws, blowing bubbles, finding age appropriate things to chew when needed.

Vision

Picture books, photos, sunglasses, sun hats, dot-to-dot games, lava lamps, reduce use of patterns in clothing and home furnishing. Follow child's preference for clothing colour and consider impact of wall and floor colours or patterns.

Vestibular/Balance

Gymnastics, yoga, crossing the midline activities (see Chapter 4 on movement), safety handrails on stairs, swinging or use of hammock, trampolining, skipping and obstacle courses.

Auditory

Whispering, humming, listening to white noise (vacuum cleaner or washing machine), songs, tapping, drumming, playing instruments, silence, earplugs or headphones.

Proprioception (body sense in muscles and joints)

Rocking, jumping, bouncing, squeezing into tight spaces, wheelbarrow walking, climbing, cycling, swimming, playing catch, gymnastics.

Building a 'day-to-day', a sensory toolkit

Every child if different; some of these ideas will help some children. They will let you know if they like it!

At home

- Mini-trampoline, Space Hopper or giant exercise ball for sitting and bouncing
- Squishing games (e.g. between two pillows)
- Swing, slide, rocking chair
- Silly putty or play dough
- Weighted blanket (expensive and might not help!)
- Learn to give a gentle pressure massage (it's basically squishing them working down from the head)
- Climbing frame
- Foot massage/back rub/hand massage
- A favourite DVD or song
- Deep hugs or sandwiching between two body pillows
- Water play area

What to do when you don't know what to do!

Out and about

- Comfortable/soothing clothing and shoes, e.g. fleece materials and Crocs.
- If your child likes public transport work with that, but the family car might provide reassurance and reduce anxiety, especially on the return journey!
- Sunglasses, hat or cap
- Ice-cold water
- Chewable jewellery/chewy snack
- Squeeze ball, big hugs on demand
- Ice-cold water bottle with a sports cap for sucking
- A comforting toy or piece of soft fabric for chewing or rubbing on hands
- Soundproof headphones
- A rough plan of how to have a quiet time/sensory break in the day
- iPad/iPhone (family life sometimes needs to go to a restaurant or café without stress!)

Example sensory diet

What works will differ from child to child, but here is an example of a structured sensory diet for a child with proprioception, vestibular and light auditory dysregulation.

Morning
Massage when waking up.
Ten minutes on trampoline.
Play involving being squished.

Lunchtime
Space Hopper at play, allow some free running.
Sensory breaks/quiet time built into the school day.
Early lunch or earplugs to help child to cope with dining hall and assembly noise.

After school
Physical activity, e.g. yoga/swimming/trampolining or den building.
Throwing and catching activity.
Calming music.
Massage.

Evening
Helping to prep and cook supper, rolling, chopping, mixing, etc.
Laying table and carrying plates.
Family activity, e.g. play dough or drawing together.

Bedtime
Warm, relaxing bath, story time in bed.
Bedtime massage, deep or light depending on child's preference.
Weighted blanket while sleeping.

A wider world of senses

The sensory checklist is an excellent way to get an overview of your child's sensory profile, but it is by no means comprehensive. Our senses are too complex to fully cover with just a few categories.

Three further processes to consider include:

Synaesthesia

The production of a sense impression relating to one sense or part of the body by stimulation of another sense or part of the body.

Oxford Dictionary

In other words, synaesthesia is a 'blending of the senses', so a person may taste colours, or a shape might have a particular smell. People can reach adulthood without realising that this issue is particular to them. Synaesthesia can be a real benefit in many professions. It can, however, also have a profound impact on a person's ability to focus on and communicate with those around them. Baron-Cohen et al (2013) found the rate of synaesthesia in adults with autism was 18.9 per cent, which was three times greater than in the non-autistic group.

Prosopagnosia

The inability to recognize the faces of familiar people, typically as a result of damage to the brain.

Oxford Dictionary

According to Barton et al (2004) up to two-thirds of people with ASC diagnoses appear to also have some form of prosopagnosia, or face-blindness. Prosopagnosia can also affect a person's ability to read emotions on faces and to detect gender or race.

Just imagine how unsettling it is not to know if the person coming up to you is a family member or a total stranger. Imagine the missed social opportunities, the energy it must take just to ask the right person for help. It would be easier, and fairly rational, to just withdraw socially and avoid social contact, without understanding that you have a biological difference, and not a personality flaw.

Alexithymia

The inability to recognize one's own emotions and to express them, especially in words.

Oxford Dictionary

The ability to recognize one's own emotions involves reading an enormous amount of sensory information and interpreting it based on knowledge of a range of emotions. Many adults struggle to do this and our kids may need more help than most to learn to pay attention to, and to read, the sensory clues to their internal state. Chapter 8, *Help me learn to manage my emotions*, outlines strategies to help kids to identify and manage big emotions.

Synaesthesia, prosopagnosia and alexithymia have been included in this section not only because they commonly occur alongside developmental delay and spectrum conditions, but also because they reflect quite how difficult life could be for our children without our realizing.

The hope here is that by understanding our child's worlds, and eventually helping them to understand their own processes we can reduce some anxiety, put support strategies in place, and help to normalize their experiences.

Experiencing the world very differently

I wanted to end this chapter with a quote from an autistic boy who has the ability to put things very clearly.

When I'm jumping it's as if my feelings are going upward to the sky. Really, my urge to be swallowed up by the sky is enough to make my heart quiver. When I'm jumping, I can feel my body parts really well, too – my bounding legs and my clapping hands – and that makes me feel so, so good.

Naoki Higashida, *The Reason I Jump*[9]

The reality is that we know very little about autism, but we do know that people on the spectrum are experiencing the world very differently to many of us. Gathering together all the information that we can and piecing together a picture of our children's sensory profiles is a big part of developing our understanding of their worlds.

Want to learn more?

Sensory integration

Research Autism view:

This intervention is highly dependent on the skills and experience of the therapist. Not all children with autism have sensory processing difficulties and careful assessment is required before commencing any programme. The research evidence which suggests that some aspects of behaviour may be helped by sensory integration-based intervention for some individuals is preliminary with insufficiently large and robust research to generalise the findings. Clear outcomes and objectives of sensory integration-based interventions should be defined at the start of therapy and reviewed on a regular basis.

Research Autism[10]

Our experience:

After several years of trampolining, rubdowns, squishing, swinging, etc., our son's sensory issues are now much reduced, or he has found ways of self-managing more of his sensory needs.

A sensory diet is surprisingly easy to slot into family life. Ten minutes of gentle wrestling or bouncing after school and just before supper is very easy to accommodate. I have no doubt that our son's anxieties would be higher were he not able to have a good run around now and again.

Recommended reading

Myles, B. and Tapscott Cook, K., *Asperger Syndrome and Sensory Issues: Practical Solutions for Making Sense of the World* (Autism Asperger Publishing Co, 2001)

Higashida, N., *The Reason I Jump: one boy's voice from the silence of autism* (Sceptre, 2014)

Horwood, J., *Sensory Circuits: a sensory motor skills programme for children* (LDA, 2009)

Synaesthesia

Baron-Cohen, S., Johnson, D., Asher, J., Wheelwrigh S., Fisher, S., Gregersen, P., Allison, C., 'Is synaesthesia more common in autism?'. *Molecular Autism* (2013)

Prosopagnosia

Visit the Centre for Face Processing Disorders at Bournemouth University: prosopagnosiaresearch.org

Barton, J., Cherkasova, M., Hefter, R., Cox, T., O'Connor, M., Manoach, D., 'Are patients with social developmental disorders prosopagnosic? Perceptual heterogeneity in the Asperger and socio-emotional processing disorders'. *Brain* 127 Pt 8 (2004): 1706-16

Chapter 4
Support my brain development through movement

Research using brain scanning has found that children on the autistic spectrum have problems with brain connectivity. There is LOADS of research on this, and on brain plasticity, so I have only included a couple of the big research centres in the *Want to know more?* section (p64).

The ideal is for your child to have occupational therapy (OT) in place. If you are still awaiting OT support we have included a range of activities that support some of the more common ASC difficulties.

One of the most often noted differences in brain connectivity in non-neurotypical kids is in the ability of one side of the brain to talk to the other. There are simple activities that can be practised at home to help your child exercise and strengthen these connections.

'Crossing the midline'

The midline is an imaginary line down through the centre of the body. Crossing the midline helps to build mental links between the two sides of the brain. Typically, young children develop the ability to spontaneously move a hand or foot over to the other side of their body, for example to reach for a toy. A lack of, or delay in the  development of this skill of crossing the midline could suggest that the two sides of the brain are not communicating well together.

If this skill does not develop it can further exacerbate developmental delays in fine and gross motor skills.

By the age of 3 or 4 most children will have mastered using both sides of the body together. Signs of delay can include difficulty putting on socks, writing, or problems using a knife and fork. If your child shows signs that they need support developing in this area there are a wide range of activities that could help them develop this skill.

Activities to encourage crossing the midline:

- catching a ball
- clapping
- yoga
- martial arts
- passing games
- throwing
- drawing
- messy play.

These activities can complement the engagement and sensory self-regulation activities in previous chapters, and again can be a part of everyday family life.

Hypermobility

There is no recent research looking directly at this area but as children with developmental delay or ASC often also have generalized joint hypermobility, it is worth considering ways to help those affected, so we have including a brief summary here.

Hypermobility has in the past been casually referred to as being 'double-jointed'. It's a fairly common, mostly harmless condition where a child's joints are less stable than usual, meaning they need to have stronger muscles than other children and will find many activities more tiring and therefore more stressful.

Joint hypermobility can have more a more significant impact on a person's life. It can affect the ability to hold a pen, sit at a table, walk long distances, climb, etc. It may also affect sleep as daytime exercise can cause muscle tightness, which can cause pain in the legs at night. ASC children who 'toe walk' are very likely to have hypermobility as toe walking can be a way of managing tightness in calf muscles.

Activities to improve muscle tone tie into the activities for crossing the midline and can be part of active, playful family life. A night-time rubdown will help to avoid muscle pain at night and can be built into the daily sensory diet.

Building functional motor skills

Building up muscle strength can also be part of the sensory diet. Squishing playdoh, threading laces and painting all help to build up muscle strength in hands.

Specially designed pen grips help to support pen grasp.

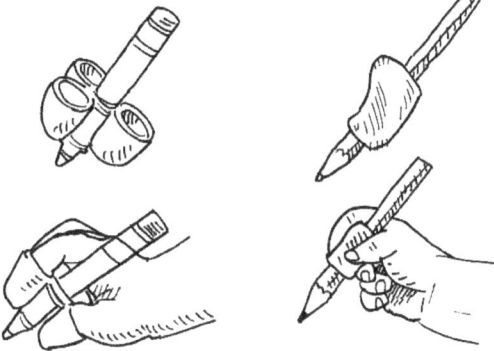

Specially designed cutlery can help kids develop the skills of handling a knife and fork, leading to improved use of standard cutlery.

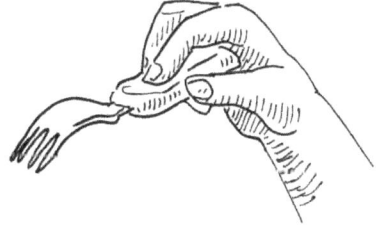

The need for these extra supports is likely to be temporary, acting as a bridge to more independent use of standard equipment. Strengthening these muscles will also help with practical tasks, such as doing up buttons, tying laces, etc., again leading to greater independence in the future.

Want to learn more?

Relationship between movement and brain development in autism

Sumner, E., Leonard, H., and Hill, E., 'Overlapping phenotypes in autism spectrum disorder and developmental coordination disorder: a cross-syndrome comparison of motor and social skills.' *Journal of Autism and Developmental Disorders*, 46, 8 (2016): 2609-20

Occupational Therapy

Research Autism view:

Please note that because it includes such a wide range of treatments it is not possible to provide a ranking for occupational therapy as a whole.

Research Autism[11]

Our experience:

OT support can be hard to get. It tends to be a one-off session where you get assessed and then get a couple of activities to do at home. If you don't build it into a regular plan or activity it could get easily lost. It can also be hard to get reluctant kids to do karate and yoga! We found family-friendly activities that we all enjoyed, e.g. swimming, Lego, gardening, etc., and just tried to do as much with the kids as we could. Using computer games, such as Wii sports, helped! (More on this in Chapter 6, *Motivation and Technology*.)

Tools for building functional motor skills

Pencil grippers

'Caring Cutlery'

Research into autism and brain connectivity

The Autism Brain Imaging Data Exchange (ABIDE)

www.sfari.org

Simons Foundation Autism Research Initiative (SFARI)

Research into brain plasticity

Green, C., and Bavelier, D., 'Exercising your brain: a review of human brain plasticity and training-Induced learning.' *Psychol Aging* 23, 4 (2008) 692-701

Chapter 5
Motivate me

Identify and work with your child's interests. An interest in dinosaurs can motivate a child to start to try to read, research, tune into others with similar interests, or to cope with a museum. Minecraft, Robots and Lego can all be great ways into topics.

Special interests as motivators

One of the many strengths of ASC kids is their ability to have intense interests in aspects of their world.

As we mentioned earlier, using your child's interests in the world around them, their 'milieu', can help you to gain their attention and expand communication through the things that interest them. It can also help you find your child's highest motivators. It might be trains, computers, animals, a trip to a theme park – anything. If it's a harmless interest it could be a reward for successful completion of a star chart. Make sure that there is a picture of the 'prize' on the star chart so that your child fully understands the connection.

It's worth noting here that the rewards can be kept very modest; an extra two minutes on an iPad or an extra trip to the park can feel like an enormous reward to many children!

Reward charts

Our kids are experiencing the world as a confusing and often unsettling place. They are frequently having to fit into situations that were not designed around their sensory needs. It's not surprising that some kids might need a little extra encouragement to take on what might appear to be run of the mill activities.

Reward systems are a technique that parents have been using for years, and they can be very helpful. If day-to-day activities are a challenge, try to identify key behaviours that if managed well will help your lives to run more smoothly – for example, being gentle with pets, staying in bed at bedtime or dressing independently.

If your child progresses well with the targeted behaviour that day give them a star (either drawn or a star sticker). Once routines and behaviour are settled you could use the chart to work on more social skills and language-based targets.

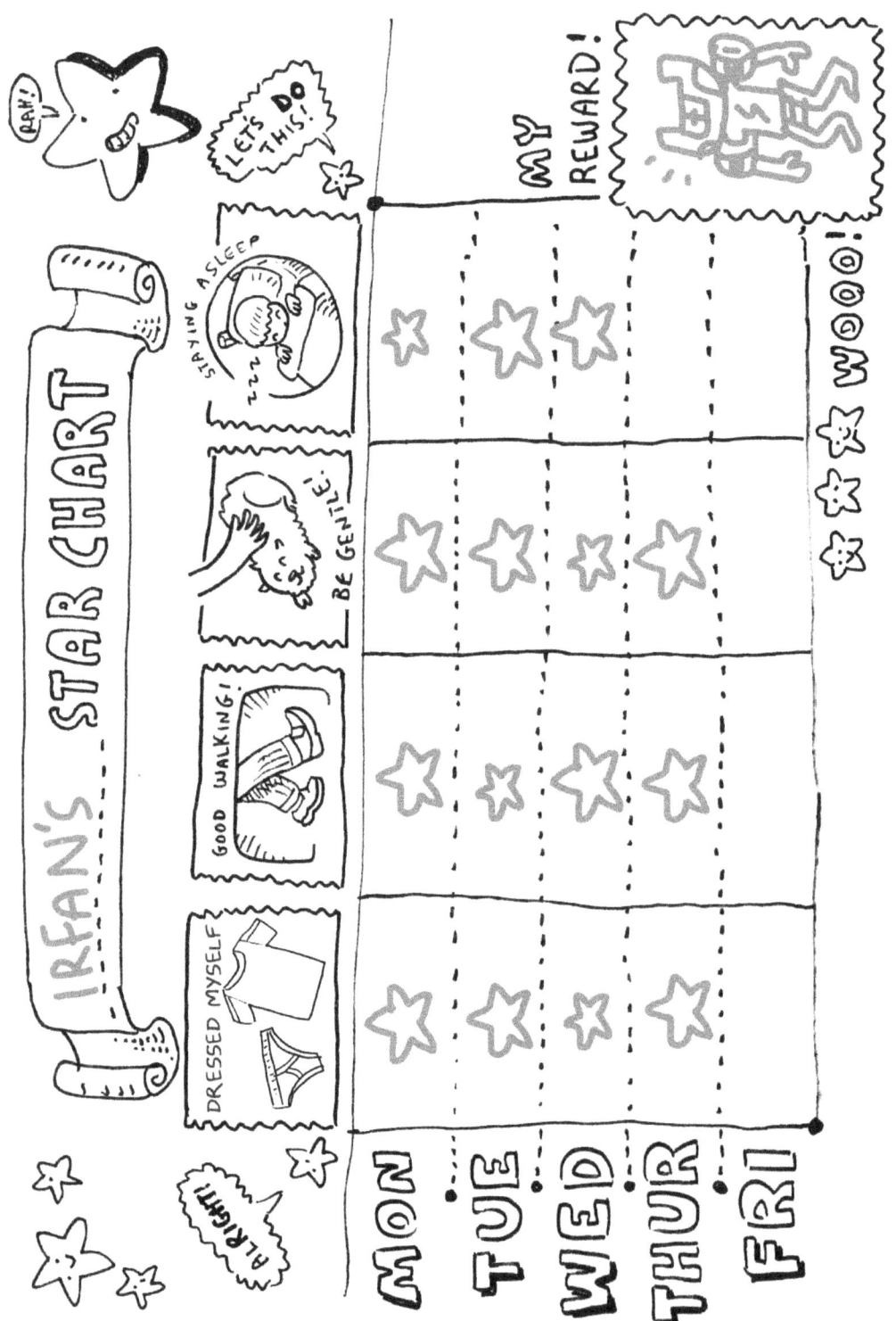

Nobody's perfect

People on the autistic spectrum can often have 'all-or-nothing'[12] thinking styles. A full week's star chart could feel like an enormous challenge if a child thinks they have to get 100 per cent of the available stars. You could make it clear that they get the reward for making the effort to achieve the goals, or that they only need to get most of the stars.

If your child worries about having gaps in their star chart you could use reward charts that allow stars to accumulate over time.

We want to set kids up to win on these reward charts so goals need to be achievable. Rewards can be agreed with the child to ensure that it is something they really want. Kids may well have worked hard to win their stars, and we want them to be valued, so they should never, ever be taken away as a form of punishment.

Pebble jars and positive-only Star Charts allow kids to see the rewards build up over time. The important thing here is that you are really clear about what the pebble or star was for. If possible give the reward the instant the desired behaviour occurs.

Kids on the autistic spectrum may well have difficulty making the connection between cause and effect so using pictures to represent the ideal behaviour, and pairing these clearly with the reward, is central to making reward systems work.

Beyond the Star Chart

Your child will make that much more effort if it gets them something they want or need. You can harness their motivation and create learning opportunities in everyday interactions.

If they need a drink, asking or signing is the way to go. Passing them the sauce at the table should be done in response to an appropriate request.

Honestly, it makes life a whole lot easier once you can see the world through their motivators. Plenty of specific praise helps to further reinforce helpful and appropriate behaviour, and is part of everyday parenting.

Also, let's face it, it can be a struggle just to get everybody ready for the day's activities. Pointing out what's in the outing for the child does speed up getting those socks on!

Want to learn more?

Milieu Training

Research Autism view:

Milieu training is a form of teaching in which the teacher takes advantage of the child's interest in the things around him, the 'milieu', to provide learning opportunities for the child.

When the child demonstrates an interest in an item or activity, the teacher encourages that interest by questioning or prompting the student.

For example, the teacher may place something that the student wants just out of reach, so that the student has to communicate with the teacher in order to get it.

There is some limited research evidence to suggest that milieu training has positive effects – usually on children's communication abilities but also in reducing aberrant behaviour.

Research Autism[3]

Star Charts

Our experience:

Star Charts made our lives work again. We started with day-to-day things such as socks on and teeth brushed. We were then able to move on to more social behaviour such as being a good sharer, or using words to tell us what he wanted. We didn't do milieu training in any depth but did find identifying the 'primary' motivator in any situation very, very useful, even if just to say, 'Let's go to the shops now so we can come back and jump on the trampoline when we get back.'

What to do when you don't know what to do!

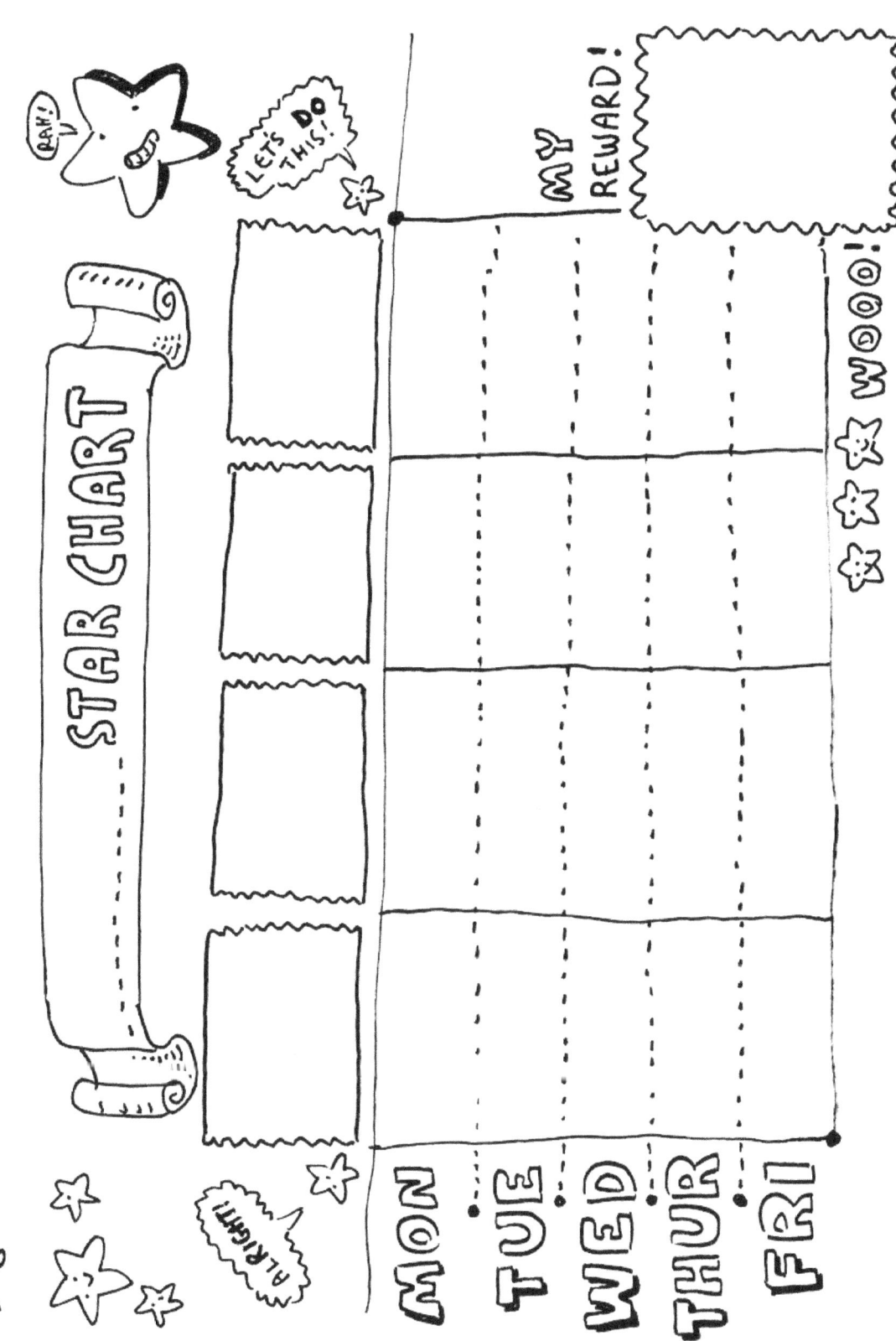

What to do when you don't know what to do!

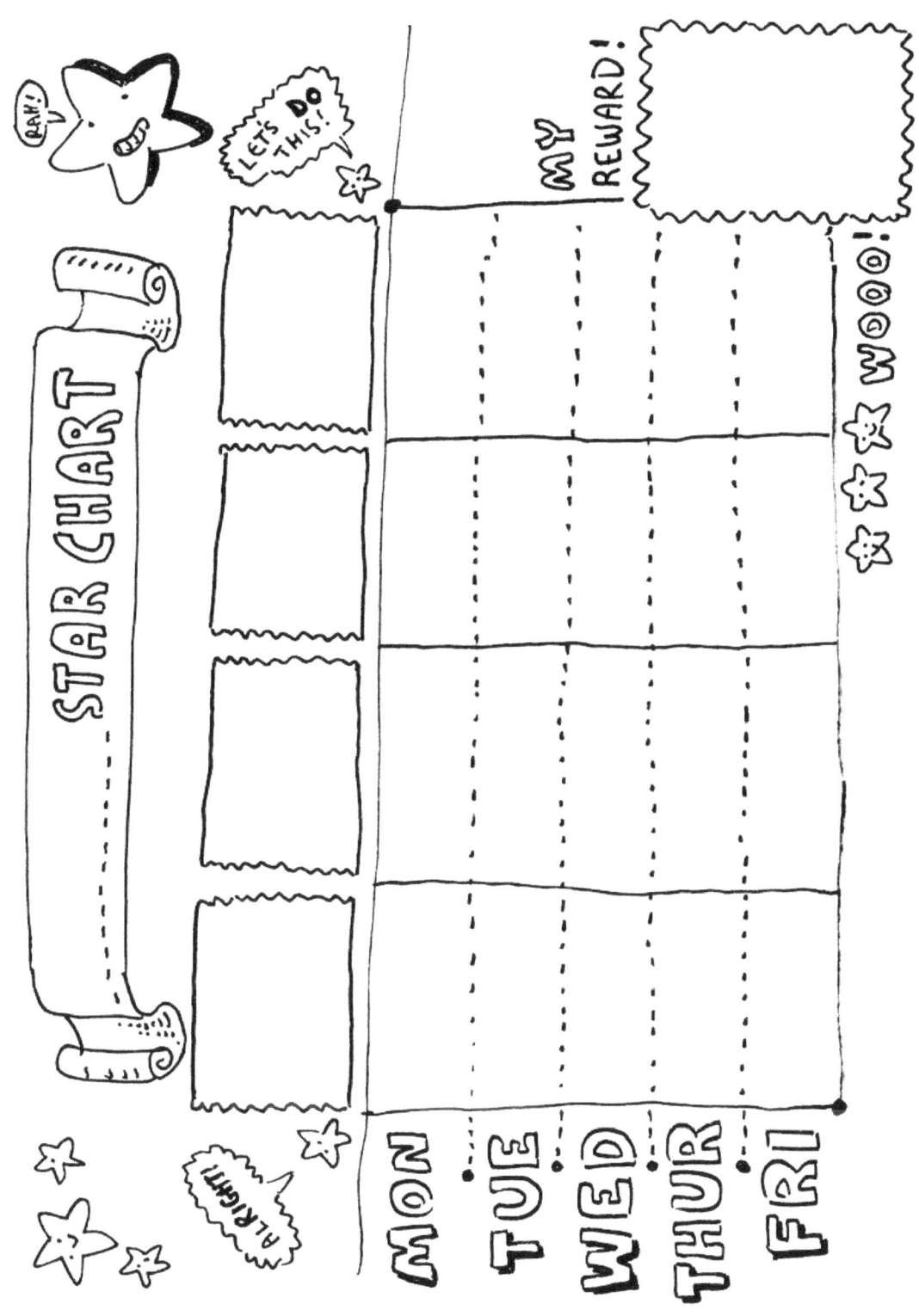

What to do when you don't know what to do!

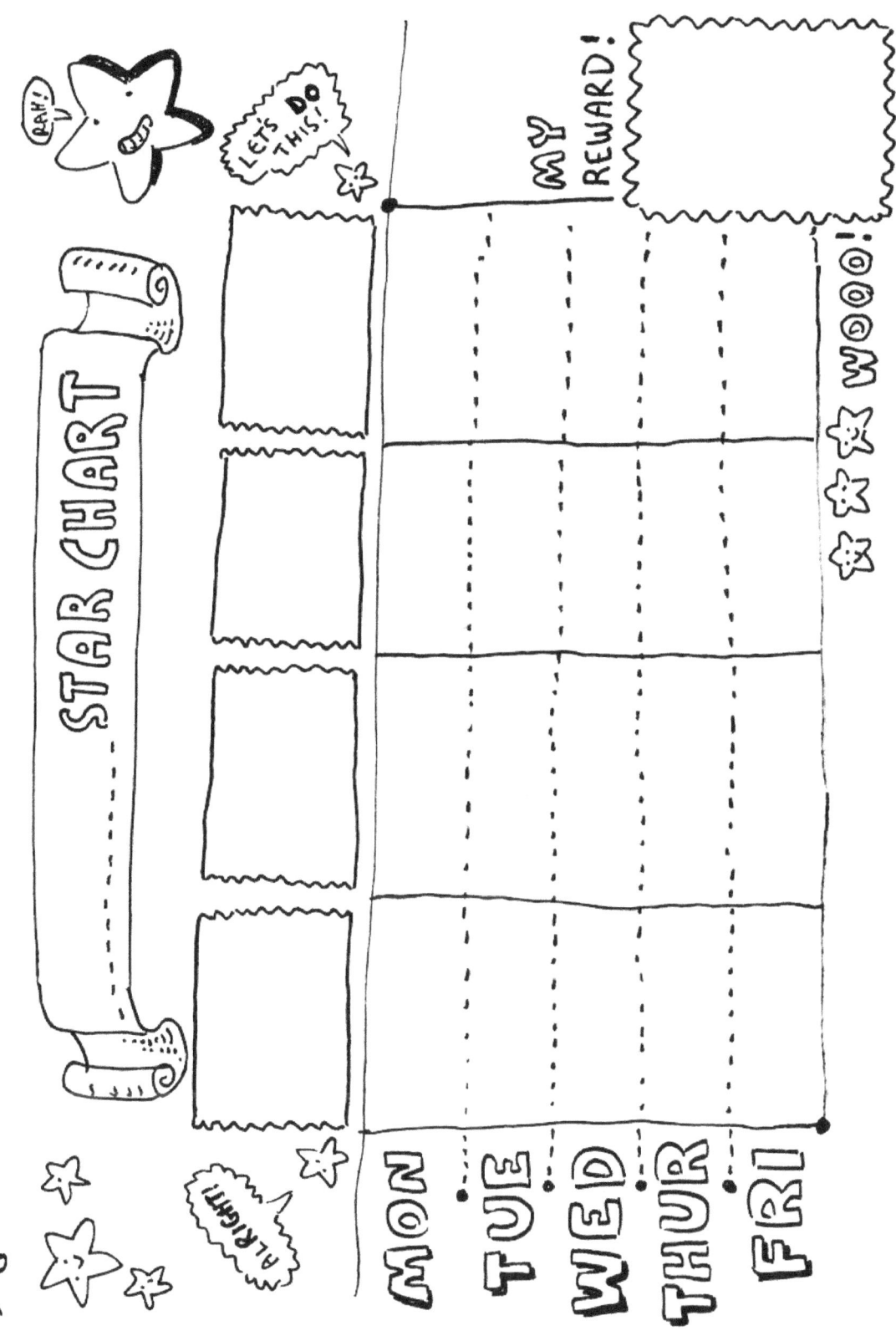

What to do when you don't know what to do!

What to do when you don't know what to do!

Chapter 6
Motivation and technology

How to use technology well is a dilemma facing most families today. Our kids get so absorbed in technology and it's a habit that can easily get out of control. Ending screen time can cause meltdowns in all children – special needs kids don't have the monopoly here.

If your child finds screens particularly rewarding, there are several points to consider.

Why technology?

Why does your child happily interact with a screen when they find the rest of the world so difficult?

Probably because they find the rest of the world so unpredictable, uncontrollable and difficult to engage with. An iPad is designed for the most accessible user experience possible. It also does what it is told and allows visual learners access to a world of information on specialist subjects. These devices have given voice to millions of non-verbal people and access to very visual learning for people who can struggle so much with processing language.

Also, looking to the future, technology might open up many areas for our children, socially and in the world of work, so it's something we should embrace…carefully.

Are they getting a healthy technology snack?

Are they watching science experiments or people hitting each other over the head? Are they playing a link up game where they and their sibling/friend have to solve a problem together, or are they playing with strangers on the net? There's a very big difference!

There are so many high quality, non-violent games and learning sites that can enrich our children's learning and development. With close monitoring, tech time can be kept as a healthy tech snack.

Screen time and overstimulation

Input is still input and kids prone to overload can still overload on technology. You know your child best: do they meltdown after 30 minutes on the device but not 15? If so, 15 minutes might be their threshold. Kids with developmental issues tend to like certainty and consistency. A definite time allowance with strict times and timers will also build a routine, which will help your child give up their device happily. Avoiding meltdowns is essential to happy family use of technology. If tech time is causing problems in your household, try a technology timetable.

Here is an example of a device time chart with ability to 'roll over' their 15 minutes per day if need be. You could also incorporate an hour long 'Minecraft Tuesday' session for the whole family.

Technology time as a social time

Curling up together with a tablet might not sound as cosy as curling up with a book but it might be an activity that your child will happily share with you. Two-player games or solving puzzles together can be opportunities for developing cycles of interaction (see Chapter 2, *Join me in my world*), especially when interaction is something your child is really struggling with.

Minecraft, Monument Valley, Pokémon GO, learning games and autism apps can all be high quality experiences that you can share with your child or your child can share with their friends or siblings.

Projects such as making animations are now easy using devices with movie-making apps, for example, Stop Motion Studio.

Sharing interests in some games can also be a form of social 'capital'.

Many ASC kids could hold a conversation on Minecraft but would really struggle on many other topics. Games can give a social 'in' to some conversations and social groups.

Want to learn more?

Minecraft (PC and most devices)

Our experience:

Minecraft changed our world as it gave our son a shared interest with many of his peers. We also learned a LOT about mods! We now have family programming projects and it's a big part of our family life. We also have a fair few movie projects. The kids do need help to set up and run these.

Technology can be a source of conflict as well as a blessing and we do have to heavily monitor when and how the kids are using it. We have needed really clear boundaries and time limits with timers. Technology has many possibilities as well as pitfalls and if used in the right way can open up a lot of opportunities for our kids.

Recommended resources (not free!)

Avokiddo Emotions (iOS)

Playful way to work through understanding emotions and cause and effect. Try to predict the animal's response to each item to help develop emotional awareness.

Toca Boca Shop (iOS)

Turn-taking fun! Two-player communication action. Amazing how bringing an iPad into a game can pique the interest of reluctant role players.

Touch Autism Apps (iOS)

From turn-taking to manners and telling jokes: delightful, effective resources.

T-Rex Toothbrush Timer (iOS)

Excellent, simple way to teach and encourage thorough teeth brushing.

Puppet Pals (iOS)

This one is very much what you make of it; excellent potential for speech and language and role play. Would need skilled supervision but could be amazingly useful.

Draw a Stickman (iOS)

Motivates children to work on their drawing/ fine motor skills. Children can draw with finger so do not have to navigate a pen to get results. The first two episodes are imaginative and gentle. The third episode, 'Epic', can be a little rougher (fighting and fire starting) and involves less drawing.

Lightbot Hour of Code (iOS and PC) and Scratch (PC)

Scratch is a free programming language and online community where you can create your own interactive stories, games, and animations. It's incredibly visual and user friendly. Anyone can learn to use this tool, you really can just follow a tutorial until your child gets the basics. Lightbox is also an excellent, accessible programming tool for kids.

Recommended reading (fiction)

Stuart, K., *A Boy Made of Blocks* (Sphere, 2016). This is a fictional account of a father bonding with his autistic son through Minecraft. The author is the father of a boy with ASC and this story will resonate with parents of kids on the spectrum.

What to do when you don't know what to do!

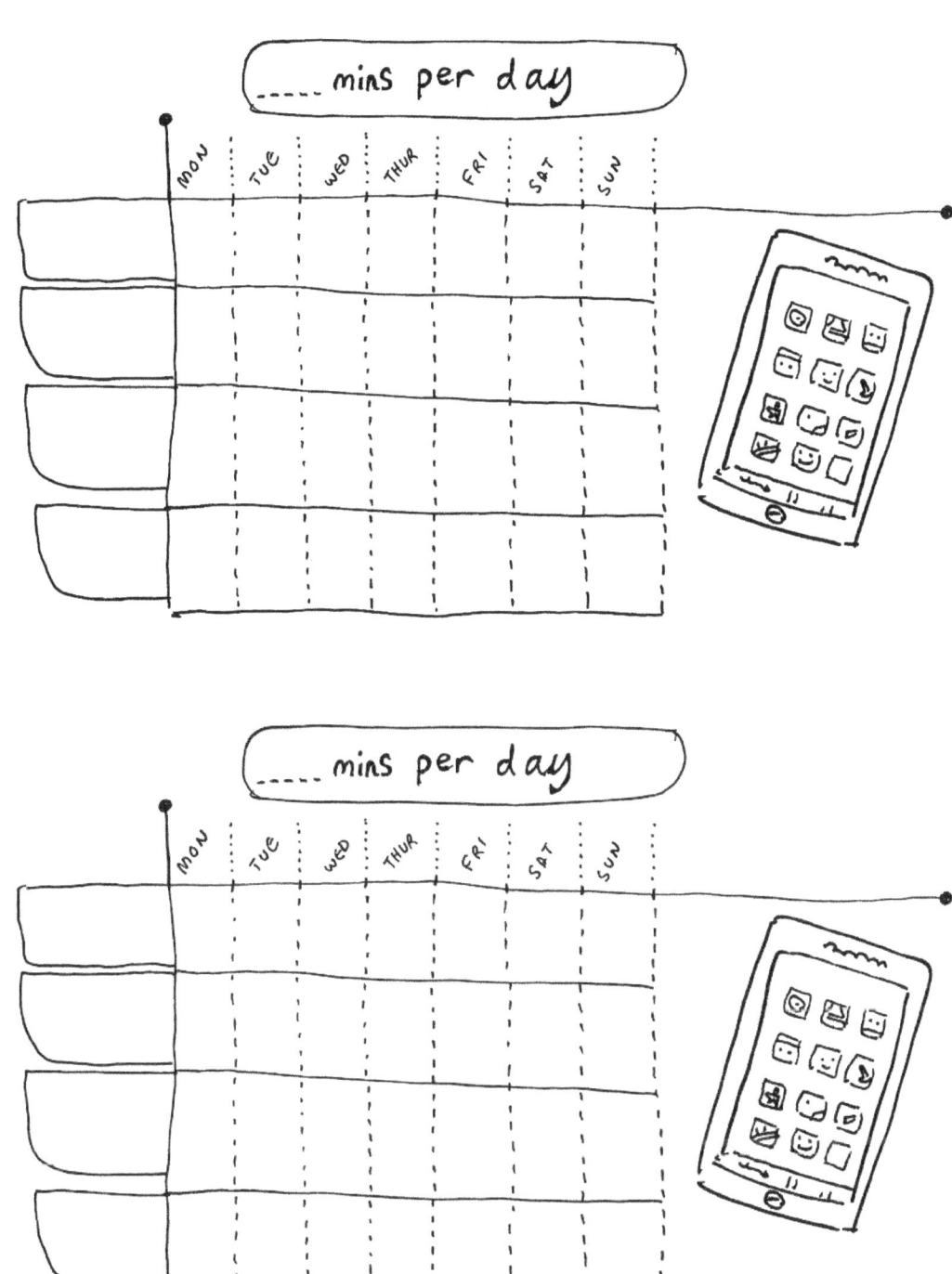

What to do when you don't know what to do!

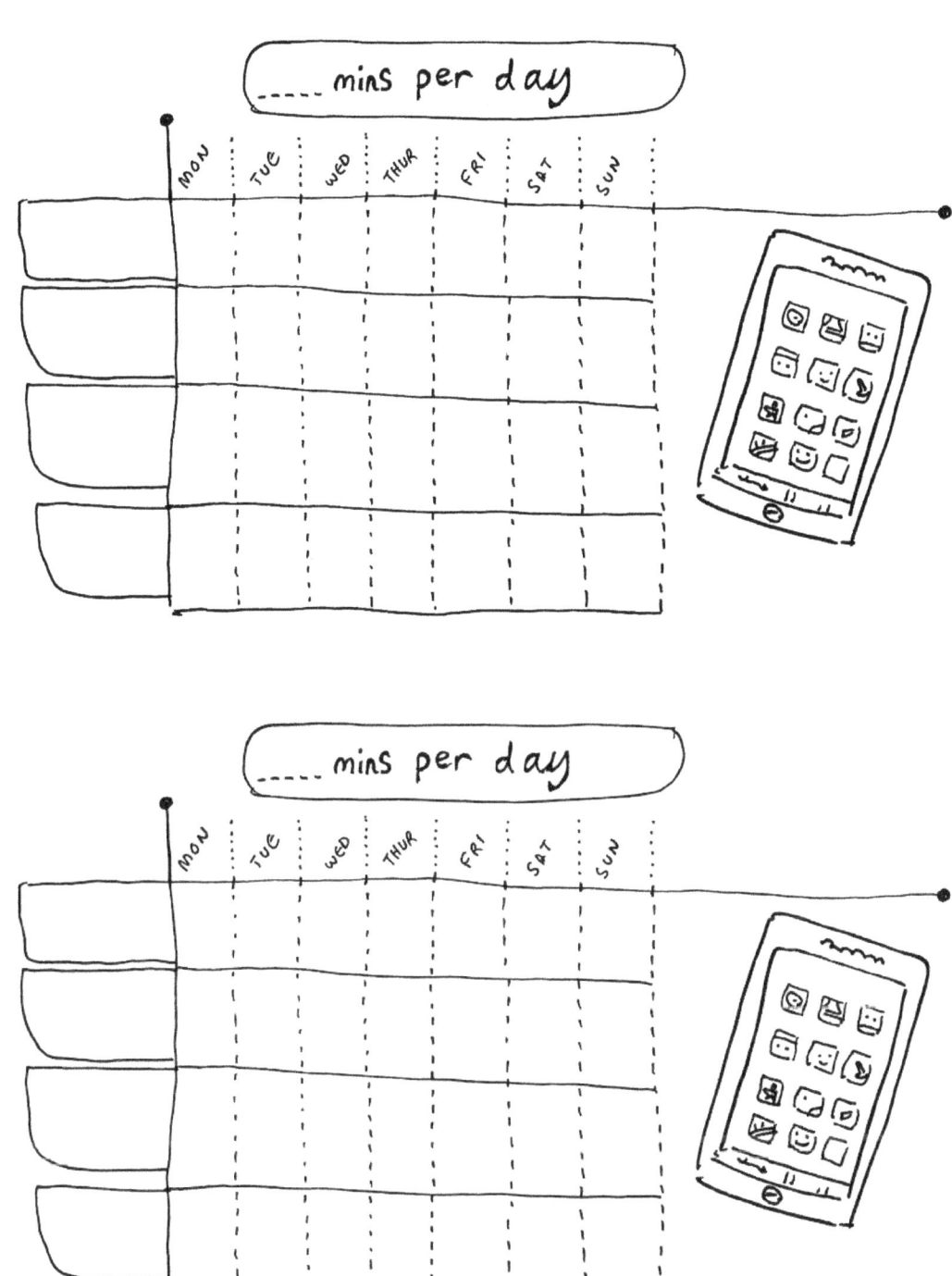

Chapter 7
My visual world

Parents want their children to be able to verbally communicate with them. Visual supports are an incredibly important stepping stone to verbal communication. Using pictures together with words will help ease your child's frustration and also support their development of language.

It can take several weeks for an intervention to show an effect or for a new behaviour to become established so we have included several copies of some resources. If you find that these resources work well for you, you could photocopy and laminate them. Use of stickers or impermanent pens on a laminated photocopy can save a great deal of time.

Useful but not essential: camera phone, printer, internet (to find pictures), Velcro strips (iron-on or sew-on), and a small laminator.

Now and Next Boards

Now and Next Boards reduce anxiety as they remove the uncertainty of what is coming next. They also help to give a clear structure to an afternoon of activities. Now and Next Boards are easy to create. Cover a piece of board or a stiff card with fabric and use it to hold the activity cards. Laminating the cards and using Velcro to attach them to the Now and Next board can be useful as it allows the child to remove an activity once completed.

You could draw your own pictures, or use pictures from magazines, your own photos, or the internet. A favourite activity in the later slot might act as a motivator for finishing a less interesting task.

Visual timetables

Visual timetables can reduce anxiety as the child can prepare for what is coming next and they know more clearly when their favourite activities will be.

You can have timetables for morning activities, the day's activities, a week at a time and/or monthly visual calendars. They will all help a child to prepare for upcoming events and feel more secure about the future. We have included samples here, which you can pull out, and if they work for you, you can photocopy them or create your own.

As with all of these resources we recommend filling them with your own visual pictures, either from magazines, the internet or your camera phone pictures printed out.

WEEK PLAN

MONDAY	TUESDAY	WEDNESDAY	THURSDAY	FRIDAY	SATURDAY	SUNDAY

Visual sequencing

Lots of children on the spectrum have a great deal of difficulty organizing information. A visual structured support will help children learn organizational skills and will help reduce the anxiety of not knowing what is happening next.

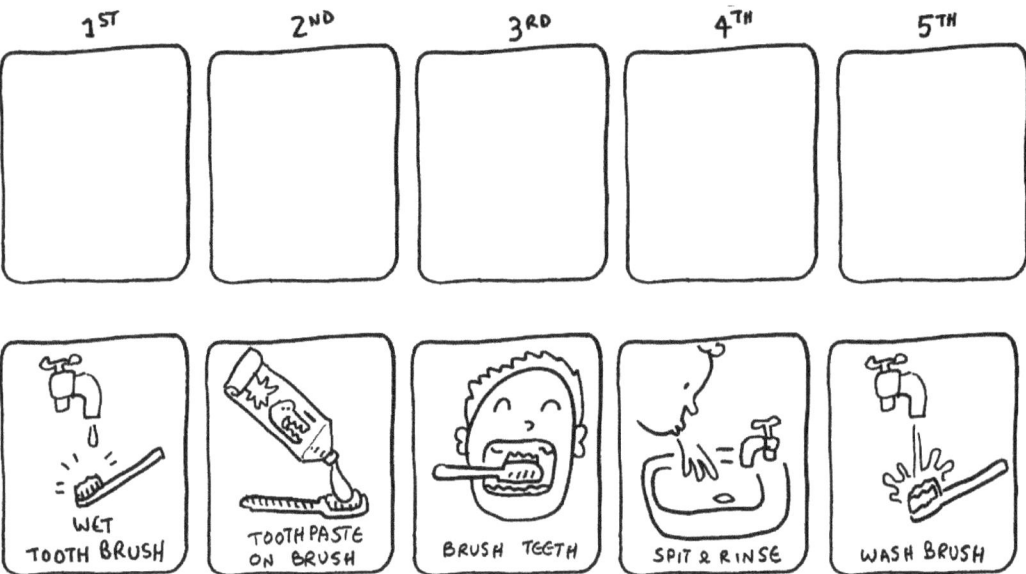

Sequence plans could be used as a visual guide to remind children what to do next or could be part of a reward chart. If you put sticky tack or Velcro on the back of each card they can be stuck to a wall or material in sequence and can be removed one-by-one when the task is completed. The child could then receive their reward or star at the end.

If you find sequence plans to be an effective way to get things done it might be worth laminating some favourite resources.

Want to learn more?

Visual schedules

Research Autism view:

There is some limited research evidence to show that visual schedules may provide positive benefits to some individuals with autism spectrum disorders by allowing them to predict or understand upcoming events.

This may allow them to reduce problem behaviours and increase their independence.

Research Autism[13]

Our experience:

Visual supports are a core part of any ASC parent or teacher's toolkit. Visual supports definitely reduce our son's anxiety. We still use a visual calendar to manage excitement and anxiety around big events. The need for visual supports has decreased but they will always be part of our lives. Many spectrum kids think in pictures so to us it's just a very rich part of ASC language.

What to do when you don't know what to do!

What to do when you don't know what to do!

What to do when you don't know what to do!

WEEK PLAN

MONDAY	TUESDAY	WEDNESDAY	THURSDAY	FRIDAY	SATURDAY	SUNDAY

What to do when you don't know what to do!

WEEK PLAN

MONDAY	TUESDAY	WEDNESDAY	THURSDAY	FRIDAY	SATURDAY	SUNDAY

What to do when you don't know what to do!

What to do when you don't know what to do!

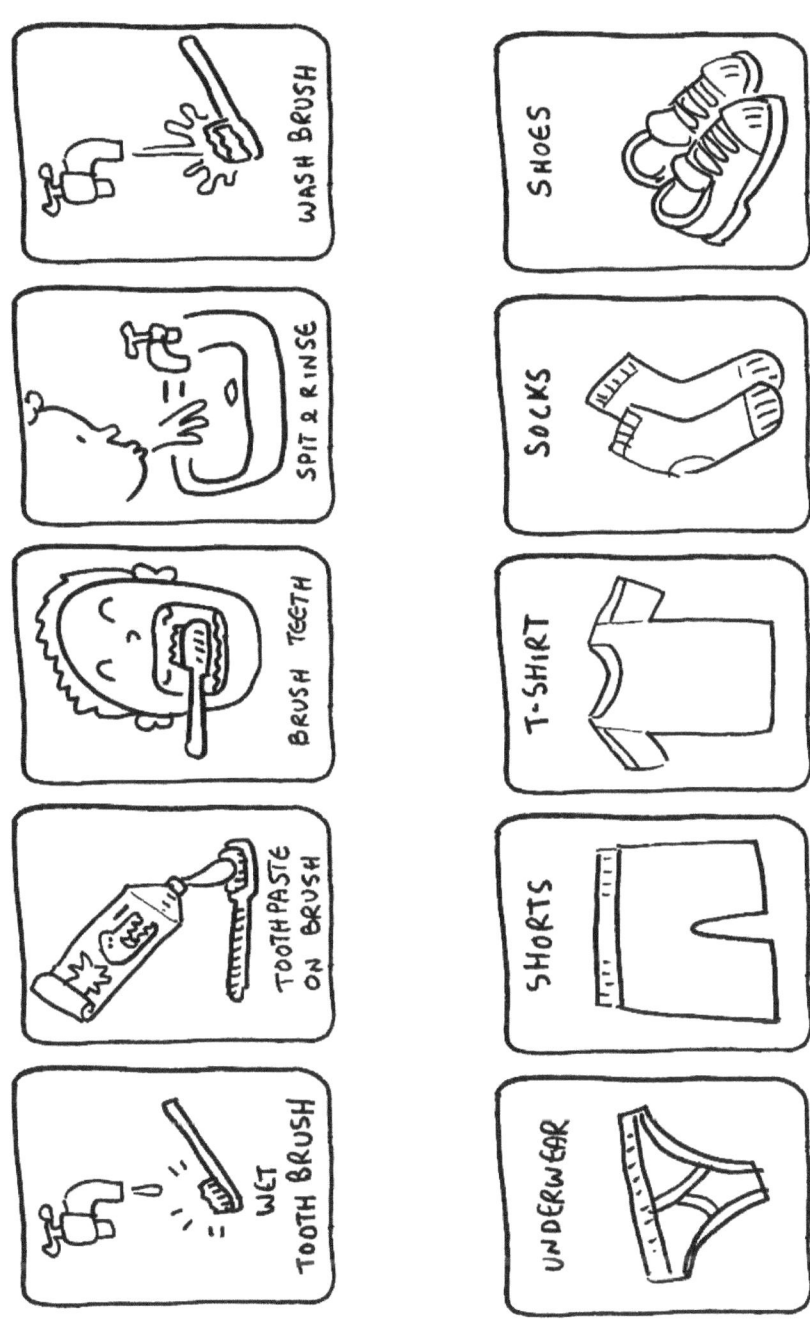

Chapter 8
Help me learn to manage my emotions

Considering the sensory overload, communication difficulties and unpredictable behaviour of other people, it's a wonder our children don't have meltdowns more often.

Whether your child is verbal or non-verbal, encouraging them to express their needs is the beginning of self-regulation. Once again, it's important to reinforce that using pictures supports development of language. Just make sure you use the language with the pictures.

Teach emotional self-regulation

This chapter will present various skills needed for emotional self-regulation. These skills build upon each other and take years to develop in all children. Our kids might need more support to develop these skills, and as visual learners they might benefit from a highly visual approach.

Encouraging your child to tune into their emotions allows them greater insight into their processes. This insight will eventually lead to the child having rehearsed strategies for times when they are feeling overwhelmed. The skills in this chapter are all steps towards emotional self-regulation.

Step 1. Teach your child to be able to identify feelings.
Step 2. Try to reflect on where in the body the emotions are felt (this skill takes time and will develop over years, but it's good to start this as early as possible).
Step 3. Use a visual scale to help identify the strength of the feelings.
Step 4. Teach strategies, e.g. relaxation, yoga and breathing techniques to help your child manage difficult emotions.

There are a lot of resources to support each step so we have included extra copies at the end of the chapter.

What to do when you don't know what to do!

Step 1. Identifying feelings

Being able to identify basic needs is a good start!

Hunger, tiredness, thirst and frustration are major causes of meltdowns in all of us. Kids on the spectrum may have greater difficulty noticing their needs developing and may suddenly be overwhelmed by a need that they have difficulty identifying.

Using visual cards, kept on the fridge, or on a keychain, can help to encourage children to identify their needs, and to make a request for their needs to be met.

Ensure that there are words as well as pictures and encourage your child to communicate their need to the best of their ability.

Move on to introduce a wide range of emotions

You could use this resource as flashcards, or you could pick out the emotions that the characters in a storybook might be feeling. It is important to encourage your child to consider feelings often. Building emotional reflection into the bedtime story routine will help to make it a regular habit in the family.

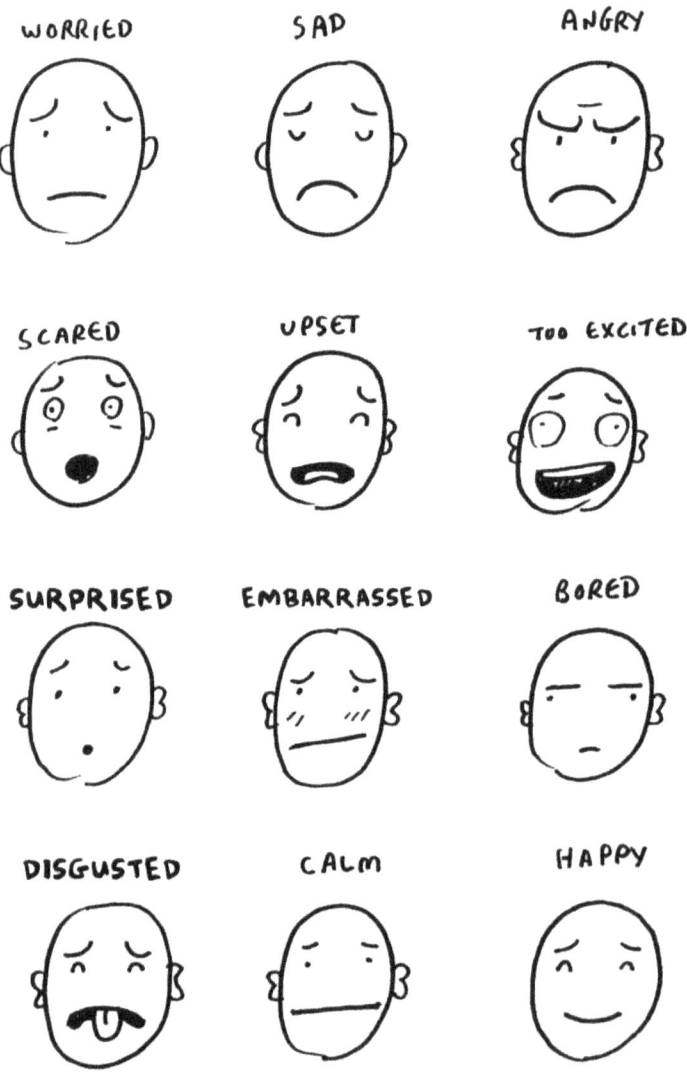

Step 2. Where in your body are you feeling that emotion?

Once a child can recognize emotions they need to be encouraged to understand the relationship between these emotions and their body.

Identifying feelings in the body is a difficult thing for many people to do so it does take time and practice.

Giving a child a blank body shape and getting them to colour in the areas that feel uncomfortable can be a good way to start.

Getting kids to visualize scanning their body from head to toes can also help to identify tensions.

Many kids feel anxiety in their stomachs and may complain of stomachache instead or identifying it as anxiety. Stress can often come out as a headache, anger can appear as clenched fists, etc.

Being able to connect the feelings with the effects on the body can give people insight into their own processes and open up ways to manage their emotions.

Step 3. **Identify the strength of feelings**

Visual scales are incredibly adaptable. There is a wide variety of visual scales available on the internet, often colour coded from a cool blue to a fiery red.

As negative emotions can have a big impact on family life we have included a scale, which might be useful in potential meltdown situations.

As with most of these resources it will be difficult to use mid meltdown and would be best introduced when your child is feeling calm and receptive to looking at things together. Following a meltdown it might be useful to talk about the triggers for increasing up the scale and what they could do differently next time.

Step 4. Develop strategies to manage the emotion in the body

Kids on the spectrum are likely to already be using strategies to help them to manage their emotions. Sensory issues and stims can be self-regulating, anxiety-reducing strategies.

Additional methods such as stretching, tensing and relaxing body parts, belly breathing strategies and massage will all help to reduce bodily tension.

Each child is unique and they will be showing you the methods that they have found help them to self-regulate. They need to understand their processes so that they can find acceptable ways to regulate when they are feeling strong emotions.

Don't forget to breathe

Blow out of mouth

Breathe in through nose

Breathing techniques, especially learning to 'belly breathe', can be incredibly effective at helping self-regulation and soothing anxiety.

BELLY BREATHING

What to do when you don't know what to do!

Eventually you will be able to use these skills together

How do I feel right now?

How are my feelings affecting my body?

What can I do to manage my feelings in my body?

Mindfulness

A mental state achieved by focusing one's awareness on the present moment, while calmly acknowledging and accepting one's feelings, thoughts, and bodily sensations, used as a therapeutic technique.

Oxford Dictionary

Breathing techniques, meditation, allowing 20 minutes per day to relax and clear your mind are all mindfulness techniques.

Research has shown that mindfulness will not 'cure' autism, but that it can reduce the frustration and negative behaviour that autism can bring.

Mindfulness techniques can be useful in improving quality of life not only for children on the autistic spectrum, but also for their parents.

Want to learn more?

As with most areas of autism intervention there is little research, and the research that there is often involves samples that are too small to allow wide generalizations; however, what research there is, is promising.

Emotional self-regulation

Research overview:

Ratcliffe et al (2014) researched Emotion-Based Social Skills Training (EBSST) and found:

EBSST improved teacher reported emotional competence. The effect size was large and improvements were sustained at 6 months follow-up.

Research in *Autism Spectrum Disorders*[14]

Samson et al (2014) concluded:

The development of treatment programs that focus on enhancing the use of adaptive forms of emotion regulation might decrease emotional problems and optimize long-term outcomes in youth with ASD.

International Society for Autism Research[15]

Mindfulness

Research Autism view:

Mindfulness training helps you become more aware of your thoughts and feelings so that instead of being overwhelmed by them, you are better able to manage them.

Research Autism[16]

Research overview:

Esther I de Bruin et al's 2014 research found that following mindfulness training:

Adolescents reported an increase in quality of life and a decrease in rumination, but no changes in worry, autism spectrum disorder core symptoms, or mindful awareness. Although parents reported no change in adolescent's autism spectrum disorder core symptoms, they reported improved social responsiveness, social communication, social cognition, preoccupations, and social motivation. About themselves, parents reported improvement in general as well as in parental mindfulness. They reported improved competence in parenting, overall parenting styles, more specifically a less lax, verbose parenting style, and an increased quality of life.

MYmind: Mindfulness training for Youngsters with autism spectrum disorders and their parents[17]

Recommended reading

Buron , K. D., Curtis, M., *The Incredible 5-Point Scale: The Significantly Improved and Expanded Second Edition* (AAPC Publishing, 2012)

What to do when you don't know what to do!

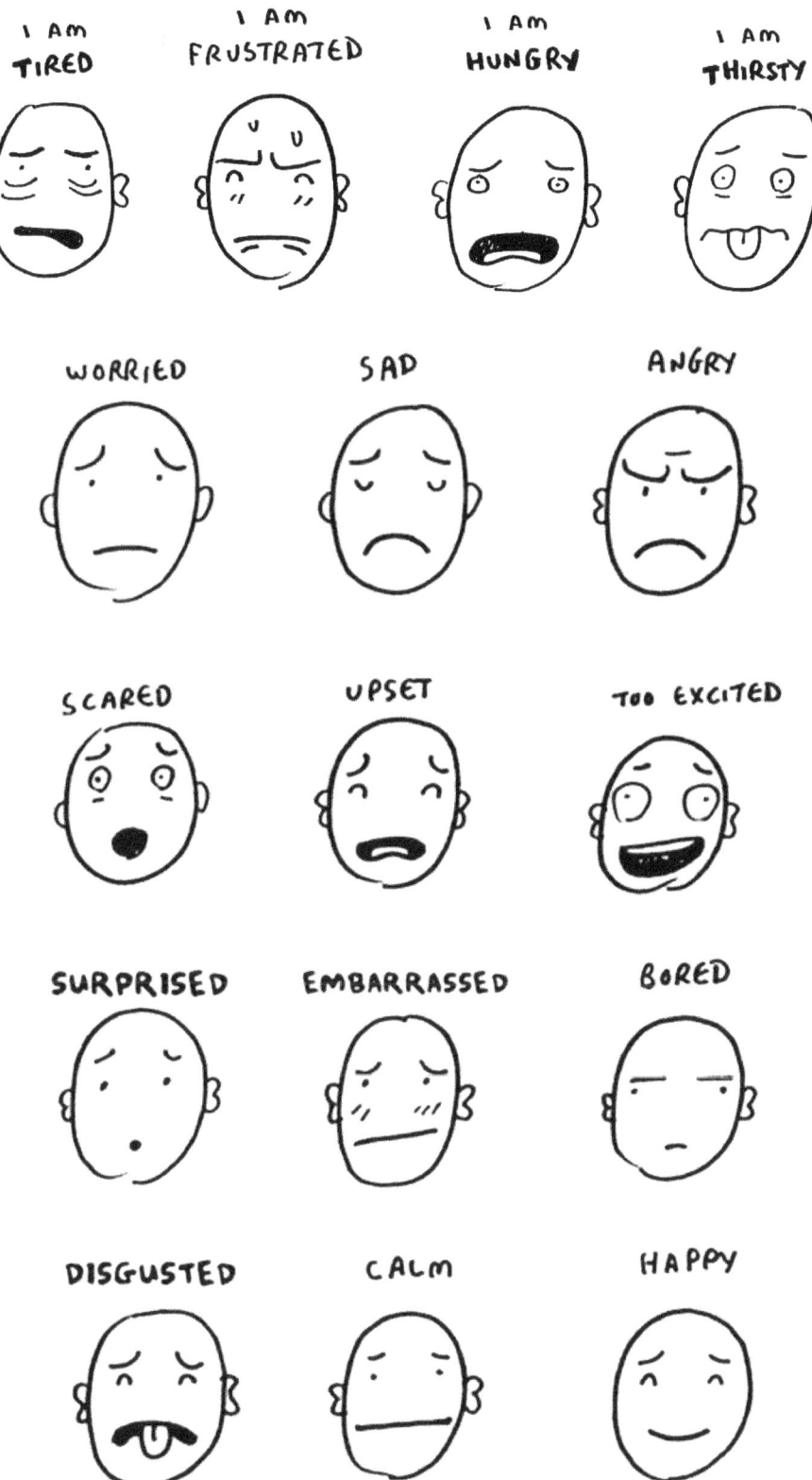

What to do when you don't know what to do!

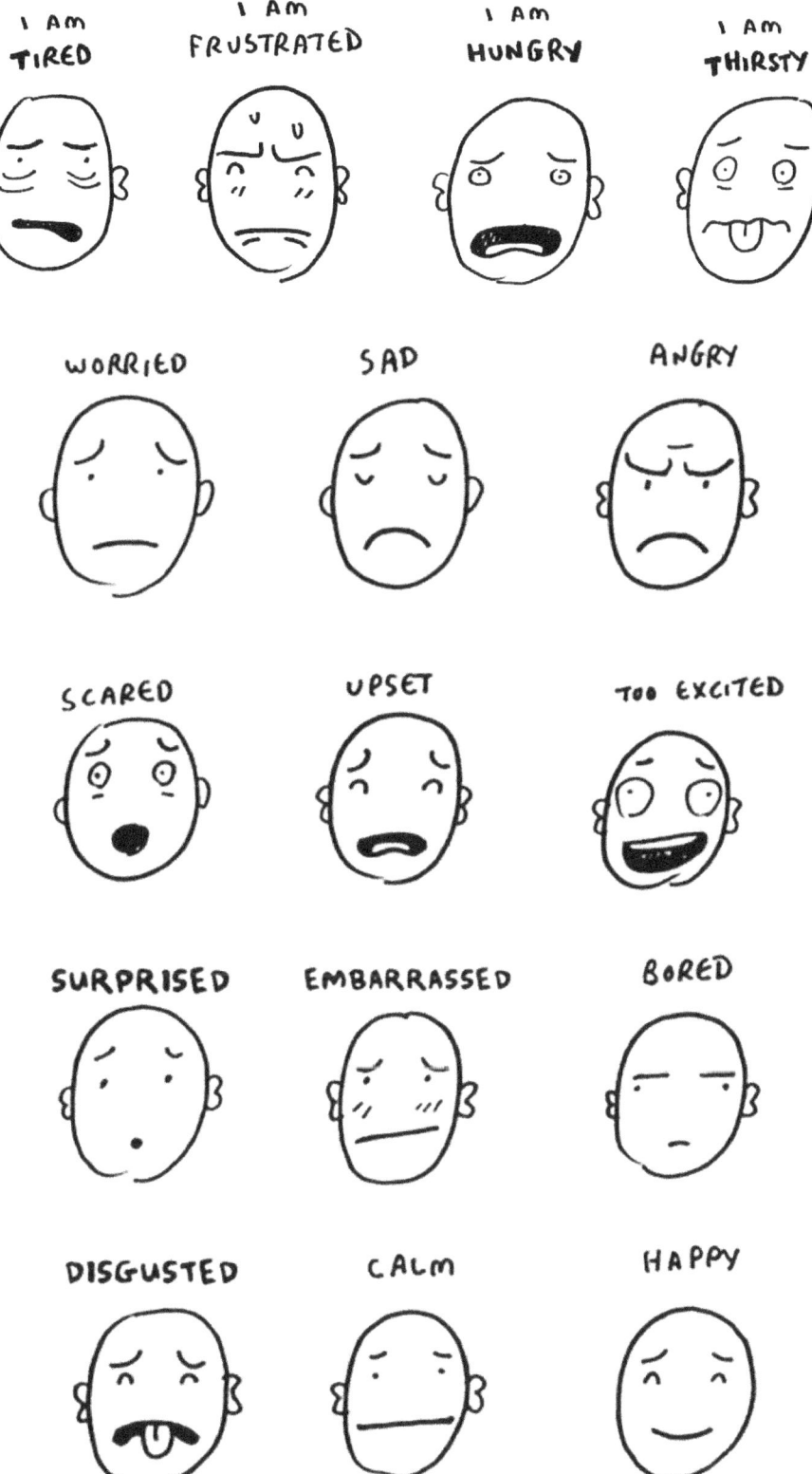

What to do when you don't know what to do!

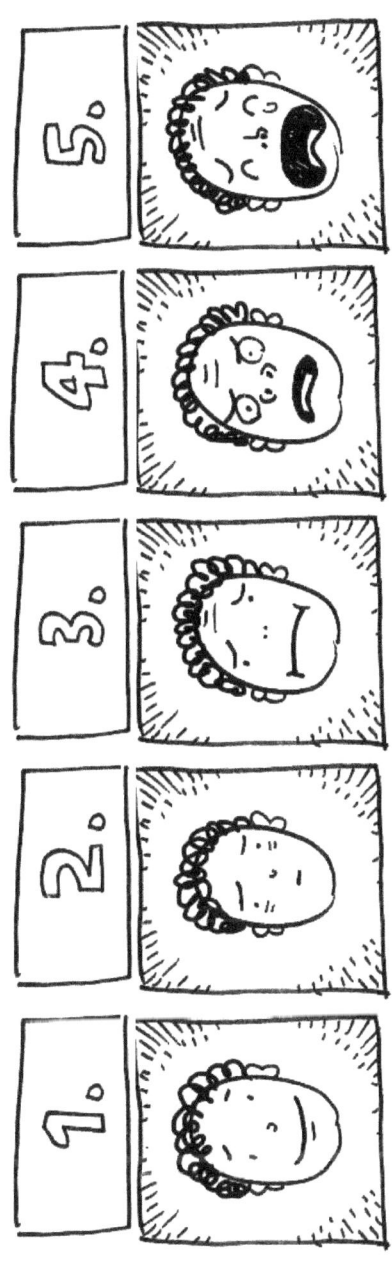

What to do when you don't know what to do!

What to do when you don't know what to do!

What to do when you don't know what to do!

Don't forget to breathe!

Breathe in through nose

Blow out of mouth

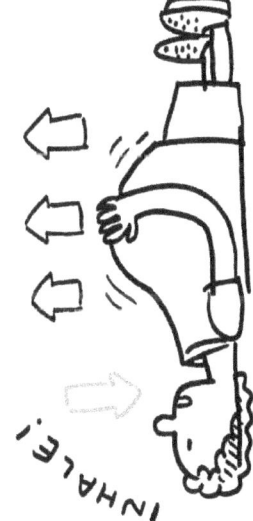

INHALE! EXHALE! INHALE!

What to do when you don't know what to do!

How do I feel right now?

How are my feelings affecting my body?

What can I do to manage my feelings in my body?

What to do when you don't know what to do!

How do I feel right now?

How are my feelings affecting my body?

What can I do to manage my feelings in my body?

What to do when you don't know what to do!

HOW DO I FEEL RIGHT NOW?

1.	2.	3.	4.	5.
HAPPY PEACEFUL POSITIVE SETTLED CALM RELAXED CONTENT	WORRIED UNSURE ANXIOUS FIDGETY JITTERY NERVOUS	SAD LOST CONFUSED UPSET TENSE INSECURE IMPATIENT	CROSS IRRITATED FRUSTRATED AGITATED OVERWHELMED DISCOURAGED UNCOMFORTABLE	RAGE POWERLESS DESPAIR ANGRY PANICKED FRIGHTENED OUT OF CONTROL

Chapter 9
Help me to develop social skills

Social skills training (SST) is a form of behaviour therapy used by teachers, therapists and trainers to help those who have difficulties relating to other people.

Some form of social skills training should be being provided at school or nursery; it could be direct one-to-one teaching, a buddy system or a circle of friends group.

While most parents are not trained to deliver therapy (and sometimes parents just need to be parents rather than teachers!), there are ways to support social skills at home through playdates.

Help me learn through playdates

Top tips for playdates:

1. Find friendly fellow parents (there are LOTS out there, but it takes a little time and a fair bit of resilience to find them). Being at the school gates helps!
2. It really helps if you know the other child quite well; it might be hard work for them at points so make sure they feel comfortable to be in your home.
3. Write out a plan for the playdate, be flexible and have some backup activities for when your child starts to struggle or needs a break. Monitor how well the children are playing and be there to step in if your child needs support to play. Be an extra playmate when needed.
4. Do try to plan activities to make sure your guest has fun, we really want them to want to come back!

Example playdate plans

- Snacks at school pick up
- Home
- 15 minutes in garden on trampoline working on ball passing (or telling jokes!)
- 20 minutes playing with pet
- 15 minutes making pizza
- 20 minutes eating
- 10 minutes hide and seek
- If going well, 20 minutes free play – if not, have an activity prepared or a game or TV show they both might want to talk about
- Send home with a slice of the pizza for Mum.

Try to keep the first few playdates short (around one or two hours). If it's a longer playdate, ending with a computer game or TV show and popcorn is not the end of the world!

If the children are playing well, totally leave them to it, but a plan is important so that you will have the activities to hand if needed!

Playdate planner

Time	Aim	Activity	Materials
3.30	Happy pick up. Make friend comfortable and feel welcome. Sharing practice.	Pick up and walk home.	Pick up snacks e.g. bananas and cheese bites.
4.00	To interact and play sociably.	Constructive play.	Lego laid out, possibly books laid out on Lego creations that they could discuss.
4.20	Collaborative play.	Den building. If support needed suggest den building with cushions, adult to support.	Cushions, blankets, chairs.
4.40	Collaborative play and interaction.	Pizza making, supported by adult.	Pizza bases, grated cheese, pasta sauce, ham.
5.00	Social eating and turn-taking in conversations.	Eating pizza. Asking about each other's day.	Dining table.
5.20	Self-directed social play.	Free play. If kids struggling to interact use back up activity of Minecraft or two-player game.	TV or PC.
5.45	Practise goodbyes and making sure they want to come back!!!!	Send child home happy with some homemade pizza.	Tin foil or pizza box.

What to do when you don't know what to do!

Friendship Skills

It is also important to help your child learn to identify what it is to be a good friend. A good friend is someone who…

Be a good friend

Friendship skills cards are great for teaching a child how to be a good friend. They can be used as a talking point, or you could pick out one or two skills to work on each playdate.

Playdates and technology

Once again, use of technology is a dilemma for all families, not just those including children with autism. The difference here is that autistic kids can really benefit if technology is used well on a playdate, particularly if they are fans of Minecraft!

There is even less research on this than on other interventions but I and many other ASC parents are convinced that Minecraft can be an excellent autism intervention!

Minecraft link up

A Minecraft link up session with one or two friends (either on iOS or on PC) can be very liberating for a child on the spectrum. ASC kids can often hold longer, more intricate conversations when focused on something that they really love. Minecraft can involve friends problem-solving together and working collaboratively, in a way that would be an enormous struggle for many ASC kids outside the game. These stronger relationships can then grow in the rest of life, too!

Staying safe online

Some servers leave your child vulnerable to strangers on the internet. We only allow local link up involving kids in the same room, either iOS device to iOS device (Pocket Edition), or PC to PC (LAN server).

Minecraft story mode

Minecraft story mode is an interactive story where players solve puzzles, fight zombies and talk to other characters to progress the story. The players choose from multiple options and direct their characters' choices throughout the game. It's a great basis for discussion as the kids can decide together the best choices for their characters. It's a nice, social alternative to watching TV or a film.

Social skills

Aside from the easier social interaction, Minecraft allows kids to understand the benefits of collaboration. We always lightly monitor the playing so that any 'griefing' (destruction/bullying) can be identified and discussed early on. It can be a really good opportunity to discuss social rules and highlight helpful behaviour.

Parental permission

Having an older, neurotypical child has helped us to have a good sense of what is appropriate, so we ask the guest child's parents if they mind if the playdate includes some social gaming on age appropriate games. No one has ever minded!

Want to learn more?

Play therapy

Research Autism view:

Play therapy refers to a large number of treatment methods, all applying the therapeutic benefits of play.

Play therapy differs from regular play in that the therapist helps children to address and resolve their own problems. Play therapy builds on the natural way that children learn about themselves and their relationships in the world around them.

Through play therapy, children learn to communicate with others, express feelings, modify behaviour, develop problem-solving skills, and learn a variety of ways of relating to others. Play provides a safe psychological distance from their problems and allows expression of thoughts and feelings appropriate to their development.

Research Autism[18]

Our experience:

Our non-autistic child clearly benefited from and enjoyed playdates so it was a very natural thing to do. Our son's social skills definitely moved on further without the distractions of the classroom, and over time he has developed some lovely friendships. Some other parents do find developmental problems too much, or are too afraid of saying the wrong thing and back away. A few years into our ASC journey we concluded it was best to be gently open and find out early if people were going to be open to our beautiful, funny child.

Minecraft

No research yet, and evidence is still anecdotal, but the presence of highly successful sites such as *autcraft*[19] (a safe server for people) are a sign that research may be worth considering!

Recommended reading (fiction):

Stuart, K., *A Boy Made of Blocks* (Sphere, 2016)

So good that I have recommended it twice! *A Boy Made of Blocks* is a fictional account of a father bonding with his autistic son through Minecraft. The author is the father of a boy with ASC and this story will resonate with parents of kids on the spectrum.

What to do when you don't know what to do!

Playdate Planner

Time	Aim	Activity	Materials

What to do when you don't know what to do!

Playdate Planner

Time	Aim	Activity	Materials

What to do when you don't know what to do!

Playdate Planner

Time	Aim	Activity	Materials

What to do when you don't know what to do!

Friendship skills cards

SHARES WITH FRIENDS

PLAYS WITH FRIENDS

LISTENS TO FRIENDS

STAYS WITH GROUP

GENTLE TOUCHES

TALKS WITH FRIENDS

What to do when you don't know what to do!

Friendship skills cards

What to do when you don't know what to do!

Chapter 10
Encouraging self-knowledge

Developing a positive sense of self

When I was small, I didn't even know I had special needs.

How did I find out?

By other people telling me I was different and that this was a problem.

Naoki Higashida, *The Reason I Jump*[9]

Your child is a person surrounded by sensory confusion, but they can probably pick up on much of what is going on around them.

Your child will be building a picture of what kind of person they are. I would recommend reading the first few chapters of *The Reason I Jump*, written by an autistic boy, Naoki Higashida, and translated by David Mitchell and Keiko Yoshida.

As our children grow they will notice that they are different from many of the other children, they will notice that their parents sometimes struggle with their behaviour and there is a real danger that they will begin to think of themselves as a problem.

Self-knowledge is a very powerful thing, and once differences are understood, they can feel much more manageable.

Examples of normalizing differences and encouraging self-knowledge

Sensory:

'Yes, that baby crying is upsetting, especially as your ears are so sensitive.'

'Yes, eggs can be very smelly, you do have a very sensitive nose! If you gently pinch your nose you won't smell the egg.'

Anxiety, novel situations:

'Why don't you want to go on the trip? When you think about the trip, how do you feel?'

'Do you know why you don't want to go or are you not sure?'

'Is it because you're worried because you don't know what the place looks like? Shall we look at a picture on the internet?'

Theory of mind (social imagination):

'I understand that you don't like it when Paul chases you. Does he know you don't like it? Does Paul have that information? Shall we tell him?'

'Sorry, I don't understand what you mean because I did not see that film, I don't have that picture in my head. Sarah might understand as she did see that film with you, shall we ask her?'

Building on strengths

You know those ASC kids who can draw amazing detailed pictures from memory, or can solve the mathematical puzzles of the universe, well maybe your child is not one of those!

But ASC kids *do* have passionate interests that we need to develop. A child's love of computer games is a route into programming; an interest in windmills can develop into playing with cogs and learning about engineering.

It's a challenge for parents, I know, but engaging with your child's interests can be fun, and can be infectious, and it also helps you join and understand their world.

Introducing your child to their diagnosis

The advice we have received has consistently been to introduce the child to their differences when they are young (around age 7). Using the terms 'autism' or 'Asperger's' might wait until the child is a little older, aged 8-10, but disclosure is recommended.

Your child will know that something is different and may have all sorts of damaging ideas about why they don't fit in, such as 'I thought I was just a bad person'. It could come as a real shock to an older child, and would be best dealt with before the challenges of adolescence. Also, let's face it, some teacher will let it slip as they will assume the child knows!

Knowledge is power and I have heard lots of stories of older children being relieved about the diagnosis as they had been thinking that they were 'just bad people'. It's a personal decision for each family.

Developing an 'Aspie' identity

We are living through a period when many of the greatest thinkers of our time are being retrospectively diagnosed with autism. With all of these positive role models, being part of the autism spectrum community may well be a source of pride for your child.

Want to learn more?

Recommended reading for parents

Higashida, N., *The Reason I Jump: one boy's voice from the silence of Autism* (Sceptre, 2014)

Notbohm, E., *Ten Things Every Child with Autism Wishes You Knew* (Future Horizons, 2012)

Verdick, E., and Reeve, E., *The Survival Guide for Kids with Autism Spectrum Disorders (And Their Parents)* (Free Spirit Publishing, 2012)

Sabin, E., *The Autism Acceptance Book: Being a Friend to Someone With Autism* (Watering Can Press, 2006)

Recommended reading for children on the autistic spectrum

Barton, M., *It's Raining Cats and Dogs: An Autism Spectrum Guide to the Confusing World of Idioms, Metaphors and Everyday Expressions* (Jessica Kingsley, 2011)

Hoopmann, K., *All Cats Have Asperger Syndrome* (Jessica Kingsley, 2006)

Verdick, E., and Reeve, E., *The Survival Guide for Kids with Autism Spectrum Disorders (And Their Parents)* (Free Spirit Publishing, 2012)

Chapter 11
Teach me theory of mind

Theory of mind (ToM), also known as 'putting yourself in others' shoes', refers to a person's ability to imagine the mental states of others. If a person has an underdeveloped ToM it leaves them very vulnerable to misunderstanding, deception and anxiety as they will struggle to predict the behaviour of others.

People on the spectrum can have ToM difficulties and can often assume others will know their thoughts. Theory of mind training focuses on teaching people how to recognize mental states in themselves and other people.

Research into theory of mind interventions suggests that these taught skills are rarely generalized, and also points out that many 'neurotypical' people have great difficulty with theory of mind.

Despite this question over the 'generalizability' of the interventions, we have chosen to outline issues and strategies for teaching your child about ToM in some depth because it is at the core of your child's difficulties.

Understanding your child's experience of the world is so important in managing not only their behaviour but also how they grow to understand and accept their own differences.

People on the autism spectrum are often presented as uncaring and incapable of empathy. An understanding of theory of mind difficulties allows us to understand why our children sometimes appear this way. It also allows us to understand their anxiety, their tiredness, and any potential paranoia.

Understanding theory of mind difficulties allows us to see that our kids can be working so incredibly hard, just to get through the day without anything going wrong.

The False Belief Test

People who have not fully developed theory of mind often have difficulties understanding other people's perspectives. This is best illustrated in the Sally-Anne False Belief Test[20].

For the child to get this answer correct they will need to be able to put themselves in Sally's shoes and understand that she did not see the ball being moved. A child on the autism spectrum is less likely to be able to imagine Sally's perspective. They may not understand that Sally has the 'false belief' that the ball is still in her basket.

Supporting development of theory of mind

Sometimes it's just useful to know where a child might struggle. Kids on the spectrum might assume that other people know everything that happens to them. Getting into the habit of adapting your language can be therapy in itself. For example, if your child talks about something you're not familiar with, such as a film they've seen, you could say: 'I'm sorry, I don't understand, I have not seen that film so I don't have a picture of it in my head. Could you tell me about it?'

Other dialogue to open up clear communication could include:

> 'I don't know about that toy, I have not seen it so I don't have a picture of it in my mind. Tell me about it.'

> 'I don't understand, can you show me?'

> 'I'm not sure what to have for pudding, what do you think we should have? What does your brother like best?'

> 'That was a funny trick, you fooled me! I really didn't expect that.'

When watching TV: 'Oh dear, do you think he expected that?'

Or: 'How do you think they felt when that happened?'

Activities to raise awareness of theory of mind issues

Hide and seek camera

Playing hide and seek is a great game to show theory of mind. The parent can show that they don't know where the child is as they did not see them hide.

If a child keeps hiding in the same place let them know that you found them because you could guess as they hid there before.

If the child does not hide all of their body it is probably because they cannot imagine what the seeker sees. Try using a phone camera to record their hiding so they can understand that they could be seen.

Boo!

Another hiding game. An ASC child may well expect a 'boo' to still be a surprise the second or third time. You can make it clear that it only works as a surprise if it is really unexpected!

Joke telling!

My dog has no nose. How does he smell? Terrible!

Jokes are often based on misunderstandings so they can teach a child that people can have more than one idea about the same thing.

It can also teach that there is a difference between playful joking and lying!

Looking at family photos

This activity encourages your child to think about their own development and growth, how they have changed and how other people see them.

Silly questions

What would the world be like if cats were in charge?

What might happen if we were able to bring back dinosaurs?

Why can't we tickle ourselves?

If our knees bent the other way, what would a chair look like?

Using cartoon strips

Thought bubbles in cartoon characters can give an enormous amount of insight into how people's minds can work. They can also be used to work through difficult situations a child might have had that day.

Cartoon communication

A picture can be worth a thousand words, especially if you think in pictures as many kids with developmental issues do!

Few people feel confident in their drawing skills, but most people can manage a thought bubble, a speech balloon and a stick-man.

Social situations and misunderstandings can be explored using pictures, for example:

Or...

What to do when you don't know what to do!

Monologuing vs. taking turns to listen and to speak

Monologuing:

Taking turns, listening and replying in a conversation:

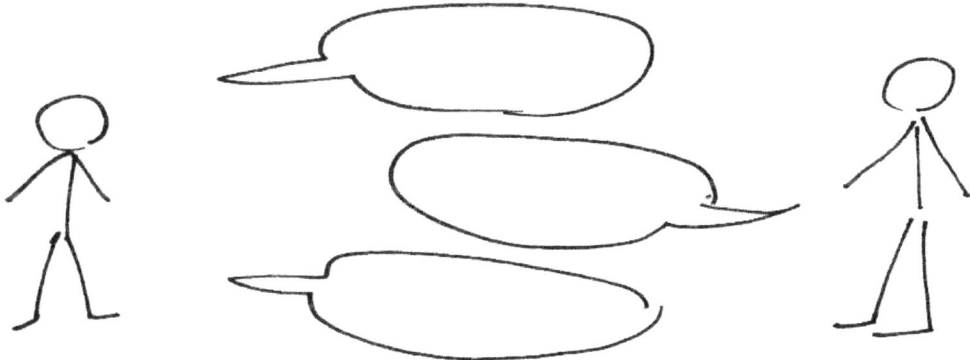

Avoiding interrupting:

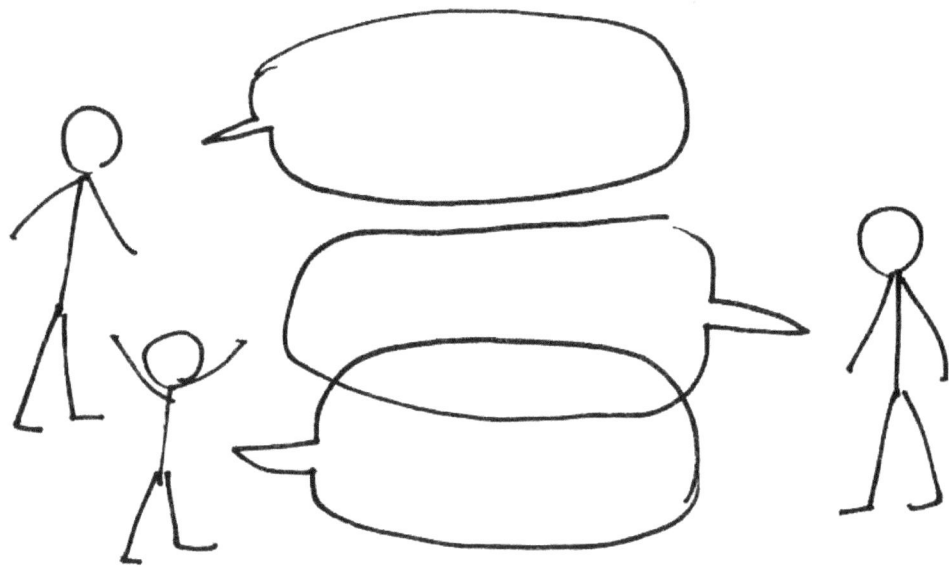

You can use cartoons to help your child gain insight into almost everything!

Expected and unexpected behaviour

Without a fully developed theory of mind it is very difficult to understand how people will respond to your behaviour. The terms 'expected' and 'unexpected' behaviour are useful as they explain people's reactions without any judgment.

It's important that ASC kids have some insight into their condition as kids can assume that they are 'just bad people' if they cause a negative reaction in another person.

The resources in Chapter 9, *Help me to develop social skills*, could be used to talk about what sort of behaviour is expected in a friendship.

Children expect their friends to talk to them and they expect their friends to stay with the group when they are doing an activity together. If a child acts in unexpected ways it can confuse the people around them, and they may be

STAYS WITH GROUP

TALKS WITH FRIENDS

less friendly as a result.

It might also be useful for your child to know that other people have difficulty with unexpected behaviour just like they do.

Films to support understanding of theory of mind

- ***Inside Out*** (Disney/Pixar). People can be independent of their feelings. Your feelings can be strong and try to influence you but you don't need to always follow them. It's good to know what your feelings are.

- ***Wallace & Gromit*** – *Stranger Danger*. Gromit has strong social instincts about the Penguin but Wallace is oblivious.

- ***Mr Bean.*** To discuss expected and unexpected social behaviour.

- ***Finding Dory*** (Disney/Pixar). Minds work differently and it can lead to misunderstandings. But it is much easier if you tell people and they can try to understand your difficulties.

Want to learn more?

Theory of Mind

Research Autism view:

It may be possible to teach theory of mind skills to some individuals on the autism spectrum using a theory of mind training programme.

However, those skills rarely or never transfer to situations outside the situation in which the training took place. It is unclear whether any skills that have been learnt can be maintained and improved on in the long term.

Because of this, researchers might wish to study other interventions (such as comprehensive, multi-component approaches) which target a range of skills designed to improve social and communication skills in individuals on the autism spectrum.

It is worth noting that some people on the autism spectrum have criticised the idea that it is only autistic people who have problems understanding how other people think. Many people on the autism spectrum believe that non-autistic people have just as many problems trying to understand autistic people.

Research Autism[21]

Our experience:

Although the research suggests that ToM is resistant to change, an understanding of ToM problems is key to so many ASC interventions that we have included it. Initially it allowed us extra empathy with our son's world, and as he has grown he has learned to know that he thinks differently and can remind himself to explain things to people. ToM is central to autism, so to us, understanding it is central to intervention.

Recommended reading

Howlin, P., Baron-Cohen, S., Hadwin, J., *Teaching Children With Autism to Mind-Read: A Practical Guide for Teachers and Parents,* 1st Edition (John Wiley, 1998)

Grandin, T., *Thinking in Pictures* (Bloomsbury, 2006)

What to do when you don't know what to do!

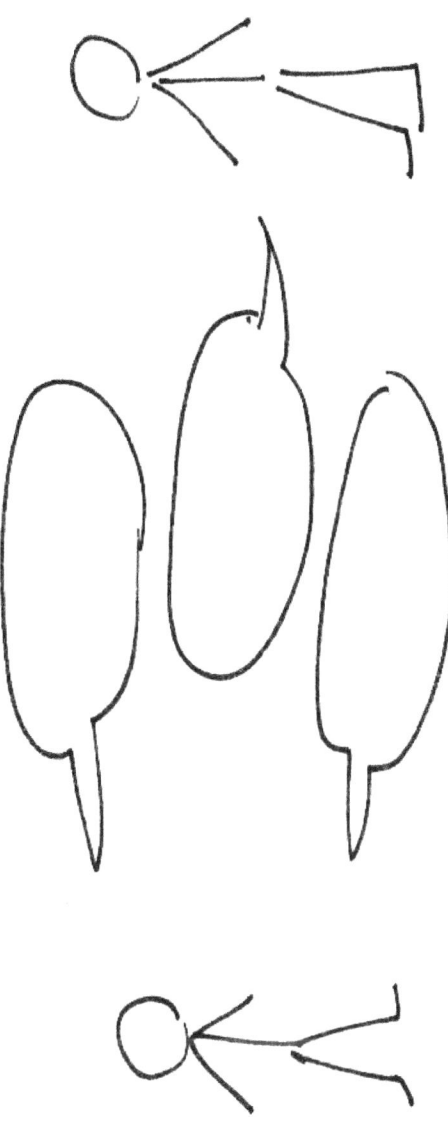

What to do when you don't know what to do!

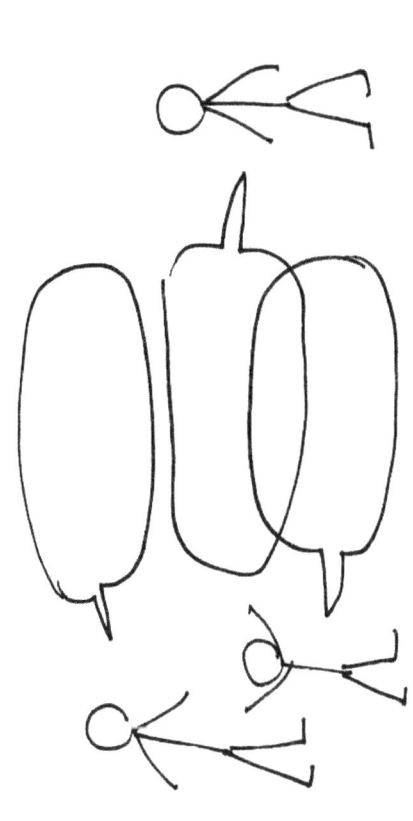
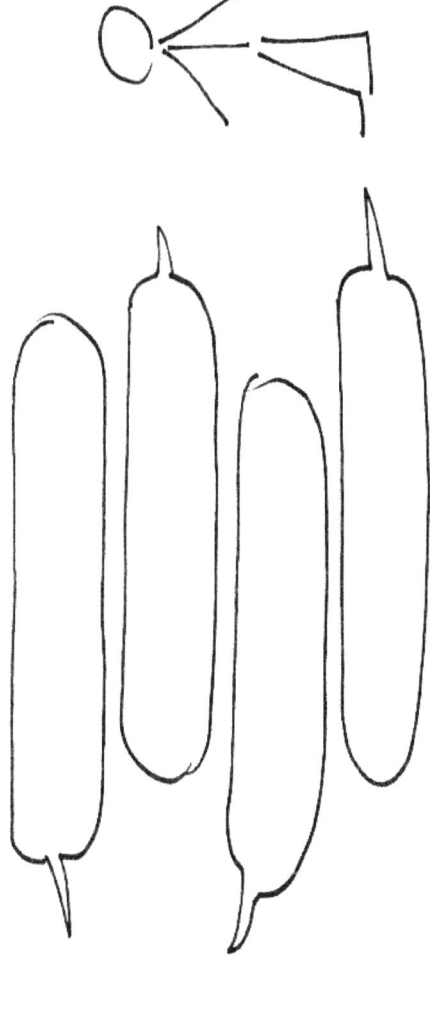

What to do when you don't know what to do!

What to do when you don't know what to do!

What to do when you don't know what to do!

Chapter 12
Care for the carers

'Autism is a marathon, not a sprint.'

Autism family support worker

Following my son's diagnosis, a local support worker took me aside and said these wise words to me: 'Autism is a marathon not a sprint, make sure you don't burn out'.

I had been attending all of the appointments, workshops and lectures, whilst trying to juggle a very demanding career in teaching, and guess what, it all got a bit too much.

Something had to give; luckily there is life after teaching and things did settle down once the pre-diagnosis worry and the intensity of diagnosis wore off.

Your child needs you for the rest of their life and while it's incredibly important to educate yourself and take steps to improve your child's wellbeing it can't be done at the expense of your own health. An intervention is unlikely to be effective if it dramatically increases your family's stress levels.

Many interventions require enormous effort and commitment from families. In this book we have tried to highlight the ones that can actually benefit the whole family unit, and not bankrupt anyone emotionally or financially in the process!

Strategies such as Star Charts and Now and Next Boards should help with day-to-day life and the sensory checklist will give you understanding which will reduce meltdown situations.

There is so much you can do, today, that will improve all your lives, but it's important to remember that we will be of most support to our children if we stay strong and healthy.

The process of adapting to the ASC diagnosis

Autism and the acceptance cycle

No one expects to have a child with a lifelong developmental disability. It is something which families adapt to over time. Autism is also so poorly understood that it can take years of researching and reading to begin to understand what life is like for our children.

Adapting to the surprise of having a child with autism is a process, and one of the most difficult times in this process is the time before and around diagnosis.

Diagnosis can come as a shock, or to some, it is a form of closure as the family can start to move on. This process also often includes grief for the child the family was expecting. Grief is natural, and does pass. If this is something that you relate to, it can be useful to recognize that grieving is happening, and to identify which stage in the grief cycle family members are currently in. You can possibly feel in many stages at once.

We have included a copy of Elizabeth Kübler-Ross's Stages of Grief cycle[21] (overleaf). You might find it helpful when considering where you and your closest loved ones are in the grieving process.

Elizabeth Kübler-Ross's Stages of Grief cycle

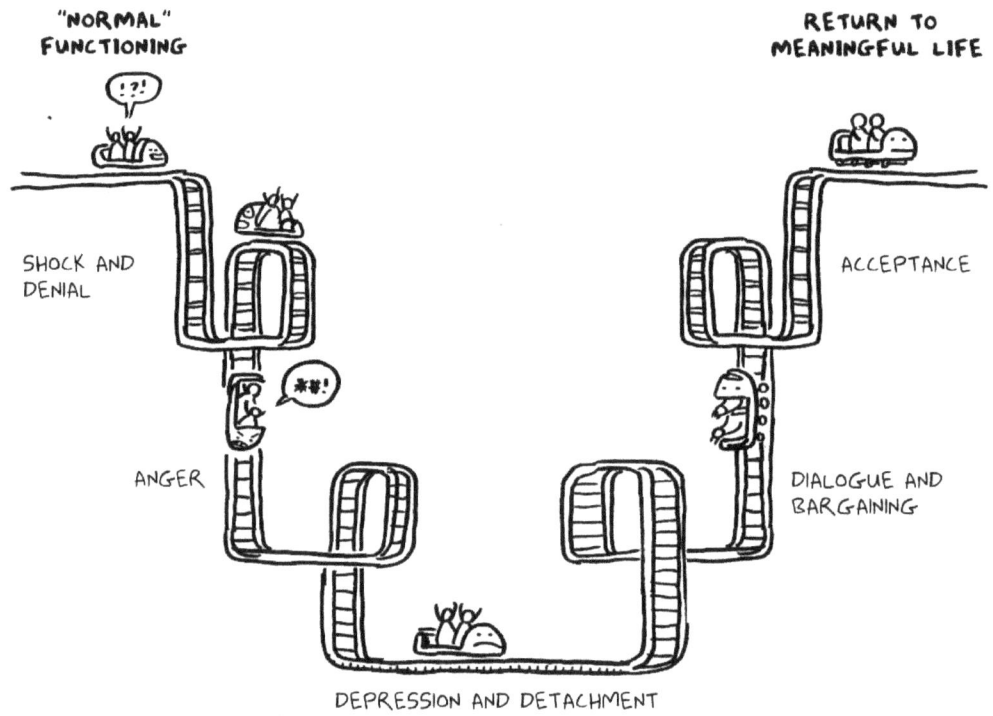

Used with kind permission of the Elizabeth Kübler-Ross Foundation.[22]

This model will not be helpful to everyone, but it could be a useful way to reflect on you and your family's processes around a diagnosis. People can get 'stuck' at particular stages, or get into cycles or loops of reactions.

Another reason for including this cycle is that if you are in a difficult stage, it is important to know that this is a process. You will adapt to this new path your family is now on, and uncover the joys of your surprising, unique child. Family life will go on and will be fully joyful again.

Take one day at a time

This is advice that we received but took a long time to start appreciating. We have no idea what the future may hold, what we do know is that kids grow and change so very much. Fear is an unhelpful emotion, and it's easy to catastrophize when the future is unknown.

Also, worrying about things that have not happened can take up a lot of energy – energy that is best spent enjoying and supporting your child.

Build a support network

We found our support network first through going to the National Autistic Society Early Bird programme[8], and then through various workshops and from other families at the school gates.

There are several reactions when we mention our child's diagnosis (and we do only mention it to potential 'friendlies'), and often the reaction is, 'Oh, my cousin/niece/sister is on the spectrum, how is he getting on at school?' Then you know there is a safe 'zone' in which to talk about ASC family life and your child's community can be that little bit expanded.

Go to autism talks, parent workshops, talk to people and arrange to meet for coffee. If there isn't a local parent support group, start one. Autism can be an invisible disability and there are many people in our communities who are struggling with similar issues to you.

Find them, it makes all the difference in the world!

Want to learn more?

This resource pack is designed to complement any support given by your health care providers. We strongly encourage families to follow an official parent training programme.

Parent Training Programmes – The NAS Early Bird Programmes

EarlyBird (under five years) and EarlyBird Plus (ages four-eight) are support programmes for parents and carers, offering advice and guidance on strategies and approaches for dealing with young autistic children. Both programmes work on understanding autism, building confidence to encourage interaction and communication and analysing and managing behaviour. The EarlyBird Healthy Minds programme is a six-session parent support programme to help promote good mental health in autistic children.

National Autistic Society[8]

Early Bird Plus is an absolute must to help you begin to learn and understand how your child's mind works.

Parent, National Autistic Society[8]

Family support organizations

Contact a Family is a national charity for families with disabled children.
www.cafamily.org.uk

The Council for Disabled Children (CDC) is the umbrella body for the disabled children's sector in England, with links to other UK nations.
councilfordisabledchildren.org.uk/who-we-are

Recommended reading

Brown, C., Goodman, S. and Küpper L., *The Unplanned Journey: When You Learn That Your Child Has a Disability* (NICHCY, 2014)

References

All references were current on October 2016.

1. Our Evaluations of Autism Interventions, Treatments and Therapies
www.researchautism.net/autism-interventions/our-evaluations-interventions

2. DIR Method and Autism
www.researchautism.net/autism-interventions/our-evaluations-interventions/49/dir-method-and-autism

3. Milieu Training and Autism
www.researchautism.net/autism-interventions/our-evaluations-interventions/91/milieu-training-and-autism

4. Intensive Interaction
www.researchautism.net/glossary/241/intensive-interaction

5. www.research.bmh.manchester.ac.uk/pactg/AboutPACT-G/NIHRpressreleaseJune2016.pdf

6. www.bbc.co.uk/news/health-37729095

7. www.manchester.ac.uk/discover/news/helping-children-with-autism-transfer-new-communication-skills-from-home-to-school

8. Parent Support Programmes: www.autism.org.uk/earlybird

9. Higashida, Naoki, translated by David Mitchell and KA Yoshikda, *The Reason I Jump: one boy's voice from the silence of autism* (Sceptre, 2014)

10. Sensory Integrative Therapy
www.researchautism.net/interventions/28/sensory-integrative-therapy-and-autism

11. www.researchautism.net/interventions/79/occupational-therapy-and-autism

12. Hare, D. J., 'The use of cognitive-behavioural therapy with people with Asperger syndrome.' *Autism* Vol. 1(2) (1997): 215-225

13. Visual Schedules and Autism
www.researchautism.net/interventions/57/visual-schedules-and-autism

14. Ratcliffe B., Wong, M., Dossetor, D., and Hayes, S., 'Teaching social–emotional skills to school-aged children with Autism Spectrum Disorder: A treatment versus control trial in 41 mainstream schools.' *Research in Autism Spectrum Disorders* (2014)

15. Samson, A., Hardan, A., Podell, R., Phillips, J., Gross, J., 'Emotion regulation in children and adolescents with autism spectrum disorder.' *International Society for Autism Research* (2014)

16. www.researchautism.net/mindfulness-training

17. de Bruin, E., et al, 'MYmind: Mindfulness training for Youngsters with autism spectrum disorders and their parents.' *Research Institute of Child Development and Education* (2014)

18. Play Therapy and Autism
www.researchautism.net/autism-interventions/types/psychological-interventions/creative-and-expressive-therapies/play-therapy-and-autism

19. www.autcraft.com/index.php

20. Baron-Cohen, S., Leslie, A., and Frith, U., 'Does the autistic child have a 'theory of mind'?' *Cognition* 21 (1985): 37-46

21. Theory of Mind Training
www.researchautism.net/interventions/87/theory-of-mind-training-and-autism

22. Elizabeth Kübler-Ross's Stages of Grief cycle. Used with kind permission of the Elizabeth Kübler-Ross Foundation. www.ekrfoundation.org/five-stages-of-grief/

About the author and illustrator

Josie Edwards is an educational resource designer, and has over 16 years' experience teaching in state schools from nursery to A-Level. Following her son's autism diagnosis in 2012, Josie left mainstream teaching to specialize in autism therapies. Josie now works closely with children on the spectrum, creating and delivering educational resources that support children through visual and kinesthetic methods. Josie also works as a designer and user experience consultant to MadeByEducators, a publishing house and educational app development studio.

Jerry Carter has many skills, amongst which is being an award-winning illustrator. Jerry has extensive experience of making educational resources for his own children and also has over 20 years' experience working in the games industry.

Jerry and Josie's youngest son was diagnosed with autism when he was four years old. They waited two very difficult years for the diagnosis and felt that there was a need for greater support for parents wanting to start early intervention.

An understanding of the challenging processes involved in special educational needs diagnosis and the difficulties in accessing support for their own child inspired them to try to be part of the solution. Jerry and Josie design resources that help their own child, and make these available to other families as affordable resources that can be used immediately, at home, and do not require costly therapists or training.

What to do when you don't know what to do!

Published by MadeByEducators

The MadeByEducators project grew from a mother/teacher seeing the potential of 'smart' devices to allow all children to access learning opportunities.

We are committed to creating accessible educational resources created by experienced specialists.

We work with SEN specialists and have a particular interest in using technology to improve the life chances of children with special educational needs (SEN).

Our books and apps are designed by teachers, with kids we know in mind, and as educators we are protective of children's privacy.

'What to do when you don't know what to do!' has been authored using pen names.

Other resources by MadeByEducators

Touch screen devices could have been invented just for children with developmental delay as they offer highly visual, responsive, fun learning opportunities. Both Josie and Jerry work closely with the MadeByEducators publishing house helping to design resources for children with special educational needs.

Many of the members of the MBE team are also parents of children with special educational needs who have a strong sense of vocation in developing effective educational resources.

These games are available on the Apple App Store, Google Play and on the Amazon App Store.

iReact is designed to help children manage difficult emotions and has been developed as a research-based collaboration between The Institute of Education at the University of London and The MadeByEducators Project.

What to do when you don't know what to do!

MadeByEducators has a wide range of Maths and Handwriting supports available. All these learning games were developed with children with special educational needs in mind. Made by Educators, tested in schools. Games with learning at their core!

Developing Handwriting Skills

Developing Numeracy Skills and using Numberlines

Times Tables and Curriculum-based Support for Mental Maths

www.madebyeducators.com

www.ingramcontent.com/pod-product-compliance
Lightning Source LLC
Chambersburg PA
CBHW081328090426
42737CB00017B/3053